D1714890

Football Coach's Guide to a

High-Scoring Passing Offense

Football Coach's Guide to a High-Scoring Passing Offense

DREW TALLMAN

PARKER PUBLISHING COMPANY, INC.
West Nyack, N.Y.

© 1975 by

Parker Publishing Company, Inc.

West Nyack, N.Y.

*All rights reserved. No part of
this book may be reproduced
in any form or by any means,
without permission in writing
from the publisher.*

Library of Congress Cataloging in Publication Data

Tallman, Drew.
    Football coach's guide to a high-scoring passing
offense.

    1. Passing (Football) I. Title.
GV951.5.T34   796.33'225   75-5887
ISBN 0-13-324053-3

Printed in the United States of America

Dedicated to
Clem Stralka
All Pro—Washington Redskins
An educator, coach, and friend to all

How This Book Will Help You
Develop a High Scoring
Passing Offense

A high scoring passing offense includes many essential facets of the game that must be totally recognized, understood, taught and drilled. In order for the pass game to be successful, all fundamentals and techniques of every position are drilled and practiced. Various pass actions should be installed. Formations, with depth and width variances, motion, shifts, and moves are necessary to understand and comprehend. Attacking each defense and its coverages thoroughly and properly must be accomplished. This book, therefore, examines all phases of a complete passing game and shows the coach how to achieve success with it.

Fundamentals of every passing quarterback action, including sprint-out, roll-out, play actions, dropback and the quick passing series, are discussed and illustrated with photographs. Receiver routes and the entire passing tree, including the quick-out, hitch, slant, square-out, post, flag, curl, turn and in, hook, etc. are totally explained, illustrated and photographed. Offensive line techniques are discussed from every pass action as well.

Strategical attack of defenses, and their coverages, is an essential aspect of every passing offense. Pass routes and patterns haphazardly picked out of a hat will not, of course, work. The offense must be able to attack defensive linebacker alignments, reactions, speed and maneuverability. Different underneath coverages of zones, man-to-man, free safety concepts and combinations are completely discussed. How to effectively attack every coverage and defender's keys and/or reads is explained in detail. Attacking procedures versus secondary coverages, i.e., invert rotation, man-to-man, free safety situations, etc. are also clearly explained and shown.

Once the coach has a total knowledge of strategical attack he can adopt the numerous pass actions and routes and form these into his offensive system. Whatever formula or system he decides upon can be geared against the defensive coverages. These varied pass actions are described in detail. The coach will have a thorough understanding on how to employ the dropback, sprint or roll-out, throwback, the quick pass, play action etc. with different methods to release one, two, three or possibly four receivers to a side of the formation. Receiver patterns and blocking combinations differ according to the style of attack, the side of a formation the receiver releases from, and the different formation variances (width, depth, etc.). These concepts are explained with each series or pass action. Utilization of screens and draws is vividly described and illustrated also.

A high scoring passing offense requires a great deal of time, drilling and practice for success to ensue. Proper employment of fundamentals, techniques, pass actions, routes, blocking and strategy are all essential. The many ideas, methods, information and techniques discussed throughout the book have been tested and used by numerous and successful teams around the country. It is believed that with the principles, concepts and suggestions presented here, the coach will be able to pass versus defensive schemes more precisely and accurately. Interceptions and incompletions will be at a minimum. This book gives a coach a thorough and complete knowledge of a high scoring passing attack. When finished he should become a good and intelligent passing strategist in every phase of the game.

Drew Tallman

Contents

9

Football Coach's Guide to a

High-Scoring Passing Offense

1

Quarterbacking a High Scoring
Passing Attack

There are many successful pass systems a coach can utilize for his offense. Some coaches like to run the ball with minimal passing. Only as a surprise element or when it is third and long will a pass be thrown. There are other coaches who will supplement their running attack with about a third of the plays being some type of pass, i.e., dropback, sprint-out, play action, screen, etc. There are a few teams throughout the country, however, that employ a pass attack as their basic offense and throw the ball over sixty precent of the time. Whatever the coach desires to execute with his offensive system it is necessary to have a pass attack that will be successful when the strategical situation arises. A high scoring passing system can be used with any offense as long as the best pass routes and patterns are executed versus defenses and their various coverages.

FIVE INGREDIENTS OF A HIGH SCORING PASS OFFENSE

There are five important segments for a pass offense to be successful. They are the quarterback, protection, receivers, coverage, and strategy.

The Quarterback

For any pass offense to be successful it is the quarterback, the passer, who must have the skill, ability and football intelligence to drive a team to victory. He must be able to get to his proper pass lane and deliver the ball on target to the open receiver.

15

Protection

A passer must have the time to set up, find his receiver and release the ball. To do this, protection by the offensive linemen and, at times, the backs is a necessity. Their ability to recognize defenses, various blitzes and stunts with the different passing attacks is important. The various techniques and fundamentals used may dictate the success they have in halting a rush of the defense. If a defender can penetrate the blockers' protective barrier, the passer will either have to hurry the release or attempt to scramble away from the tackle. Each extra second a passer has available increases the percentage of completed passes that can occur.

Receivers

The ability and skill of an offensive receiver is the next important ingredient of a sound pass attack. He must be able to align with proper width according to the pass being executed. He should release from the line and get away from any defenders attempting to hold him up, run the proper route called versus the defense shown, and catch the football if it is thrown to him. If he has any speed, he should be able to turn upfield to gain any extra yardage needed. The receiver is now a ball carrier trying to maneuver toward the goal line and outrun the opponent.

Coverage

Once the pass is in the air everyone sprints to the spot where the ball was thrown. The passer should tell ''left,'' ''middle,'' or ''right,'' which indicates to the team, especially the protection, where the ball is located. The reason for this coverage is twofold. If the pass is short and caught by the receiver, there will be extra blockers in the area for the receiver to utilize; and if the ball happens to be intercepted, the passing team will be in position to tackle the interceptor.

Strategy

Strategy is by far the most significant single aspect of a pass offense. This is especially true after the techniques of the pass game are taught, drilled, and accomplished. Strategy includes using proper formations of width with respect to the quarterback action or receiver route used. Then various pass patterns can be executed versus the defensive schemes used. It is necessary that the coach install well conceived passing patterns to take advantage of the opposition's pass coverage and weaknesses. Some passing patterns may or may not be as successful against certain coverages. Throwing at the improper time or executing poor pass routes will nullify all the work put into a well organized pass attack. For a good passing attack to be successful the quarterback and receivers should be properly taught and drilled on the routes and patterns executed.

Reading coverages *before* and/or *after* the snap of the football is an important strategical part of a pass attack. The quarterback, ends, and backs must be able to read. Reading is used to attack defensive weaknesses that occur just prior to the snap versus certain defensive formations. If this cannot be done then reading the movements and coverages once the ball is put into play must be executed. Reading is employed in order to get a completion, cut down on mistakes, avoid interceptions, and have the best passing percentages versus the coverage used. It is utilized to achieve the best patterns and to get all receivers open as quickly as possible.

THE QUARTERBACK AND HIS OFFENSE

There are many varied pass offenses a coach can adapt. It is highly recommended that a coach use the size and ability of his quarterback personnel for the pass offense he desires. For example, there is quite a difference in the throwing aspects of a sprint-out to a drop-back attack. The following are a few of the talents a quarterback must possess in the different pass offenses.

The Drop-Back

To pass from a pocket, as a quarterback would from a drop-back, it is desirable that he have good height to scan over the heads of the offensive line's protection. Speed and quickness are not altogether necessary to get to the passing position. However, he can set up and read open receivers better if he possesses them. Different footwork patterns may have to be experimented with to get the quarterback to set up quicker. He must have the patience and experience to stay within the pocket for protection as long as possible, and then be able to quickly step up and away from the pass rushers when necessary. A quick release and a strong passing arm are essential. He should be able to throw to the left, middle and right and at all depth and width routes. According to the passer's ability, a coach must design patterns for the quarterback's release mechanism and strength of his throwing arm. Shorter receiver routes may be of necessity to some quarterbacks while others can throw medium and deep patterns easier.

The Quick Drop-Back

The quick (3-Step) drop-back pass is a relatively short pass attack. The set up is quick by the quarterback and the receivers can run four or five quick routes. Fundamentally, this is an easy pass to complete for any quarterback. However, if the wide-out receivers (split ends and/or flankers) split at any great distance a long pass could result. He must have a quick release. Fast footwork, setting up and throwing immediately are important. Height is not necessary since blocking can be altered to assist him.

The Sprint (Roll) Out

A good sprint-out or roll-out quarterback should have speed to attack the corner. Height is not necessary since most of his blockers will be low going after the defensive rushers. He should have practice, experience and ability to throw the ball with accuracy on the run. He may have to run with the football if his receivers are covered and, therefore, he should be a good ball carrier.

The Throwback or Semi-Roll / Semi-Sprint

When a quarterback sprints (rolls) behind his guard or tackle on either side of the center he is attempting to pass to the front or backside depending upon the design of the pass or defensive coverage. In either case, the quarterback must have the style of a drop-back passer since he will have to look over the linemen's heads and throw various medium and long routes. If the quarterback doesn't have a strong arm, short and/or delay type patterns must be developed.

The Quick Sprint-Out

The quick sprint-out attack is similar to the quick drop-back in terms of pass routes except the quarterback is running in the direction of the receiver. In this case, the pass itself will be shorter and, therefore, the quarterback does not have to possess as strong an arm. Height, of course, is not especially significant, but throwing quickly on the run is necessary.

Combination of Each

The best pass offense a coach can utilize is a combination of each pass attack. If a quarterback is talented and he can learn, understand, and execute both the drop-back, sprint-out, and variations of each, then the offensive attack can create a great deal of pressure on the defense. This helps in achieving success against various pass rushes, blitzes, containment, and secondary/linebacker coverages. Of course the quarterback must be tall enough to throw in a pocket, but fast enough to attack at the defensive corner and run if the occasion occurs.

Play Action

While most teams have play action passes, it is the coach who has an inefficient passer that can utilize them the most. In attempting to outmaneuver secondary coverages, play action may force both linebackers and the secondary to react in the wrong direction. By forcing the defense to jump to a play fake the quarterback has the best opportunity to get an open receiver and complete the pass. If the quarterback does not have any "zip" on the ball or has a poor release, a play action pass will definitely assist the offense.

ESTABLISHING THE PASSING GAME

There are many questions that must be pondered and then answered in setting up and building a complete pass attack. Some of the necessary questions to keep in mind are the following.

1. How good is the quarterback's ability to pass the football with accuracy? Can he deliver the football at the precise moment it is needed with minimum interceptions?

2. Is the quarterback a sprint or dropback type?

3. What are the strengths and weaknesses of the receivers? Are they tall, short, slow, fast, quick, shifty, etc? What kind of ball carrying ability do they possess? Can they catch the hard thrown ball? What is their experience and understanding in executing pass routes versus zone or man-to-man? Who can catch the long "bomb" or short pass constantly?

4. How good are the offensive linemen? Some linemen are better with the dropback game because of their strength and physical size.

Other linemen are better to aggressively attack as in sprint action because they are smaller, but quicker.

5. Is the quarterback knowledgeable and experienced enough to call the proper formations, motion and pass action to effectively attack the pass defense strategically?

6. Can the passing game be effectively coordinated with the running game in order to help both attacks? Successful running plays can extensively assist good play action passes and vice versa.

7. Is there enough time within the practice schedule to effectively execute and establish an excellent pass attack without jeopardizing the running phase of the offense? A good and varied passing game must be worked and drilled to be successful. The more passing used—the more time needed to practice it. A coach must understand this if success is to be found with a passing game.

8. What effect does passing have on the running game?

A high scoring passing attack can greatly supplement the running phase of the game. The more wide open the attack an offense can sustain, including all formations, motion, patterns, etc., the greater the pressure of coverages and rushes placed on the defense.

QUARTERBACK SKILLS

With the different passing games that can be installed into an offense, there must be certain quarterback fundamentals and techniques instinctively established so pass plays are executed and gain success. Each aspect of the pass attack should be drilled properly every day of the season, with emphasis placed on correcting the errors that occur. By eliminating errors each time they occur, the passing game will become more efficient.

Quarterback-Center Ball Exchange

Receiving the football from the offensive center is a matter of habit beginning from the first day of practice. There are many methods of snapping the football. The ball can be hiked with a quarter turn, half turn, flipped completely over from point to point, etc. No matter what procedure is adopted by the coach, the quarterback should receive the football with the laces at his finger tips so, as he pulls away from the center, he is prepared to throw the ball immediately. Photograph 1-1 indicates the hand and finger relationship with the football.

Quarterback Stance

Different stances can be used by the quarterback. The feet can be parallel or with a toe-heel relationship. A staggered stance with one foot slightly ahead of the other is another method. Foot placement will be dependent upon the type of offense employed, including the various running and passing phases. The knees should be slightly bent for push off ability, with the back arched forward and head up. Weight should be distributed on one of the feet so a quick push off in the direction needed can be accomplished. The hand placement is very important. The thumbs should be in contact with each other with

Photograph 1-1

*Center-quarterback hand-finger relation-
ship using the ½ turn snap.*

Photograph 1-2

*Hand placement for the snap of the foot-
ball.*

Photograph 1-3

*The quarterback's stance—notice the bend
of the knees, arched back, and head position.*

the outside top portion intergrooved with the lower portion of the thumb of the
other hand as shown in Photograph 1-2. Photograph 1-3 indicates the quarterback stance.

Quarterback Footwork

Since there are various passing actions, different footwork patterns must
be used for each one. The footwork execution will be explained with each
passing attack (dropback, sprint-out, roll-out, etc.). Diagram 1-1 indicates the
various actions or paths the quarterback can use.

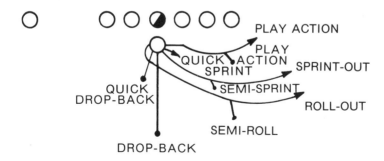

Diagram 1-1

Deep Drop-Back Techniques

There are fundamentally three ways a quarterback can step back on the dropback pass (7-9 yard depth). They include the following methods.

1.   The Cross-Over Step
2.   The Back-Pedal
3.   A Combination of the Cross-Over and Back-Pedal

1. The Cross-Over Step

Once the ball has been snapped, the quarterback will push off with his left foot (a right handed passer) and get as deep as possible with his right foot, which is usually a 3 foot step. At this point the shoulders turn perpendicular to the line of scrimmage, the hips are opened up facing the sideline, and the right foot is positioned at a 45 degree angle from the neutral zone. The first step must be placed directly behind the left so an exact backward line of depth can be obtained. If the first pace was not positioned directly in back, the cross-over of the second step can not be made. With this open step position the quarterback should be directing his eyes upfield for any type of reading of linebackers, secondary and receivers. The ball should be brought up to chest level near the passing shoulder, with the left or opposite hand used to stabilize it.

From this first maneuver the body will use a flowing motion to obtain the depth necessary. The second step crosses in front of the first as deep as possible. When this is accomplished, the arms and hands shift the football across the chest to the non-throwing arm. This makes it easier to run or maneuver backwards. As the third step is taken, which is in direct line with the second step, the ball flows toward the passing arm again. A fourth and fifth step is now made to complete the required depth. A sixth and seventh step may be necessary if the coach desires. However, at all times the eyes must be focused on the passing areas with the shoulders perpendicular to the line of scrimmage. The depth will be determined by the length of the steps of the quarterback, and 5 or 7 steps may be employed. The fifth or seventh step is the stopping or planting foot, which is the right foot of a right handed passer. As the foot is planted, the quarterback should dig in the turf hard and bring his opposite foot almost next to it. In this position the quarterback is standing straight and tall and looking downfield. The cross-over technique is shown in Photograph 1-4.

2. The Back-Pedal

The footwork of the back-pedal is completely opposite that of the cross-over and slightly slower for the passer to get depth. The quarterback takes the snap and begins to "run" backwards. The ball is brought to the chest and the shoulders remain parallel to the line of scrimmage. The eyes, of course, continue to scan downfield. The footwork is quick, snappy, and short step movement. The number of steps will vary according to the depth desired. Once the depth has been reached the quarterback can set up, ready to pass as explained previously. Many coaches desire this footwork because the quarter-

Photograph 1-4

The dropback pass with cross-over foot-work. The hips open toward the sideline, the ball is positioned at chest level and the eyes continually scan downfield.

back can read linebacker stunts and utilize the "hot" receiver principle. If a designated linebacker stunts, the quarterback can immediately pass the ball to a receiver that theoretically should be open. This is explained in detail in Chapter 7. The back-pedal technique is indicated in Photograph 1-5.

3. A Combination of the Cross-Over and Back-Pedal

This style of footwork is rarely seen, but has been used successfully. It is utilized to hit the "hot" receiver, but if not used, a quicker drop or more depth can still result. If a quick pass is necessary, the quarterback takes the snap from center and immediately begins to backpedal and read linebackers. If on the fourth or fifth step he notices that the linebackers are not blitzing, he will immediately turn his shoulders, open his hips to the sideline and begin to employ the cross-over pattern.

Quick Dropback Techniques

The same fundamentals and techniques that applied to the crossover step and/or back-pedal on the dropback pass can be used for the quick dropback

Photograph 1-5

*The dropback pass with the back pedal
footwork.*

passing game. However, a 2 to 3 step maneuver is adopted, and the quarterback will set up and be prepared to throw the ball.

The Quarterback Sprint-Out Pass Footwork

The open step or face out is utilized with the sprint-out pass. The quarterback pushes off the inside portion of the left foot (if sprinting to the right)
and pivots the right foot into the direction of travel. This first step is "thrown
out" and short. As this step is taken, the ball is brought up by both hands to
the passing shoulder and the eyes focus on the receivers. The ball should be
ready to throw on the second step.

Although the methods employed to move away from the center are a
matter of individual preference, the idea is for the quarterback to arrive at his
anticipated area under good controlled speed. A depth of 4½ to 6 yards behind
the tight ends position should be reached. Five steps are usually necessary to
get behind the tackle's position and six to get behind the end, although this
may vary.

As he reaches the end's position, the quarterback will immediately turn
upfield facing his receivers. The shoulders should turn parallel to the line of
scrimmage so he can pass the ball anywhere upfield (left, middle, or right).

The quarterback's footwork is not tight or sharp, but is rounded. Common quarterback mistakes include getting too much depth, causing an exaggerated curve in the route. Being too shallow on the sprint-out is another mistake. The quarterback's footwork is illustrated in Photograph 1-6.

Photograph 1-6

The sprint-out pass footwork. Notice the ball is ready to be thrown on the second step.

Semi-Sprint-Out Techniques

The semi-sprint-out pass is used by teams that desire to show the defense a sprint-out look. However, they will stop short of the offensive end's position, set up in a pocket around this area, and throw either front-side (toward the sprint) or throw back. The same initial footwork patterns and ball control are used as in the sprint-out. However, on the fifth or sixth step the quarterback will immediately stop, set up, and look to his pattern side, reading secondary and linebacker coverages.

The Roll-Out Footwork

The roll-out techniques of the quarterback are similar to the sprint-out pass except on the initial 2 steps. The quarterback will achieve a little extra depth as he clears the center also. If the quarterback is moving to his right, he

Quarterbacking a High Scoring Passing Attack

will use a reverse pivot technique. The right foot is utilized both to push away from the center and to pivot. The left foot is brought back and around, then planted in the direction desired. The ball is brought to the stomach, with the front of the body temporarily facing the direction opposite that of the intended line of flight.

As the second step is taken, the quarterback will snap his head around and immediately look downfield for the pattern called. On the third step the ball should be ready to throw. This entire action should be approximately a 45-degree angle from the line of scrimmage. His route and course will be similar to the sprint-out pass except he may be slightly deeper. The first few steps of the roll-out are shown in Photograph 1-7.

Photograph 1-7

The Roll-Out Footwork

Semi-Roll-Out Pass

The reverse pivot is exactly the same as the roll-out. However, as explained with the semi-sprint-out, the quarterback pulls up somewhere around the tackle-box area at 4½ to 6 yards in depth prepared to either throw front-side or back-side according to the pattern called.

THE ART OF PASSING THE FOOTBALL

Passing the football with accuracy is considered the most important aspect of a high scoring pass threat. If the football cannot be delivered to the receivers, there is absolutely no sense in passing the football. It is significant to realize that passing the football with accuracy and good acceleration *can be taught* to almost any player who prefers quarterbacking. However, proper drills, teaching techniques, practice time and experience are all necessary if a quarterback is to excel. Strength and throwing quickness may have to be developed also. However, a player can learn, through a prime and qualitative football program, to pass the ball with a good degree of non-error if he and the coach work at the correct techniques, fundamentals and coaching points. The action of the pass, as will be explained, is shown in Photograph 1-8.

Photograph 1-8

Passing the football from the ready position to the follow-through.

The Ready Position

Whether the coach decides to utilize the drop-back, sprint-out, roll-out or a combination of these attacks, getting the football into a position so it can be released quickly is vitally essential. A receiver may be open at any time and the wise quarterback will be ready. The ready position will enable him to get the ball into passing position quickly, causing quicker and more accurate passes. In the ready position, the passing hand has the ball in the proper location with the fingers on the lacing. The other hand is placed on the bottom portion and used only for guiding and supporting. The ball is positioned by the neck and passing shoulder. Both elbows are completely bent and rotated up and away from the hips. A few common mistakes by inexperienced quarterbacks are to have one hand on the ball (it could be dropped), lowering the ball so it has to be brought up to throw, stationing it too high so it is in an uncomfortable position, etc.

If the quarterback is stationary, as in a dropback, semi-sprint, or semi-roll, the body should be facing the sidelines with the weight balanced and shoulders perpendicular to the line of scrimmage. The eyes are scanning downfield, and the quarterback is ready to accurately pass the ball. However, if the quarterback is on the run, he must learn to utilize the ready position while on the move. More practice time, therefore, should be emphasized to pass the ball while running.

The Passing Position

The passing position begins when a receiver becomes free in the secondary. This is accomplished through reading of secondary or linebacker play and/or quarterback and receiver timing of a particlar pattern. Once the quarterback decides to pass (a practiced reaction), the ball should be brought into a passing position with the slight assistance of the opposite hand. In one flowing motion the weight is shifted over the passing foot, but automatically begins to flow to the opposite foot with a slight foward jab step being executed. As this is done, the hips will naturally slide forward with the weight shift. However, the shoulders and arm should remain in their original position, and an essential dip of the shoulder can be executed so a slight arch is completed with the passing shoulder, rib cage, and hips. Weight is now placed on the forward leg. The ball is brought above and behind the passing ear and may be adjusted somewhat higher. The ball is cocked slightly upward at this point.

Passing Action of the Arm

Once the ball and upper torso is cocked to throw the football, the action of the shoulder becomes important. At the fraction of a second when the ball is to be thrown, the shoulders should rotate back to assist the arm for strength in acceleration. The chest muscles act to enable the shoulder joint to rotate the upper arm toward the midline of the body. The elbow is held above the shoulder in a natural position away from the body. The flowing movement of the shoulder and upper arm to the midline of the body furnishes the starting force of the pass. The upper arm remains almost parallel to the ground, with the elbow always above, never being lowered or pointed toward the ground.

The movement of the forearm from behind and above the ear is initiated at the instant the elbow is almost, but not quite, pointed toward the receiver. The forearm is snapped out toward the receiver for quick acceleration; it is flexed fully and extended rapidly with force. The wrist plays an important part just before extension is reached. The wrist rotates medially with the hand, turning outward toward the receiver. The palm is facing him. The wrist snaps downward for added acceleration. The fingers coordinate with the wrist and release the ball with a downward force. With this rotation the palm and thumb point toward the ground, and the forefinger aims directly at the receiver. This snapping action of the fingers creates a downward force on the back end of the ball, causing it to spiral with the nose up.

The shoulder, upper arm, forearm, wrist and fingers coordinate in a single, quick and flowing motion. The body should lean forward for the follow-through.

The Follow-Through

Once the ball is in the air, the quarterback should yell in what direction the ball was thrown. Such words as "left, right, and center" designate where the ball is located. The offensive linemen will then cover in the direction called. They are now in a good position to tackle any defender if the ball is intercepted, or to help block for the ball carrying receiver.

Passing on the Run

The same passing action is used when passing the ball on a sprint or roll-out course. However, once the ball has been released, the quarterback should continue to "run after the ball." With the passing arm still extended, the quarterback continues toward the receiver. The arm should never come across the body as with a baseball pitch.

The quarterback must learn to throw the ball while running. He may have to release the ball from either foot, which can be difficult if not worked upon. When the ball is to be released, the shoulders must turn toward the receiver or become parallel to the line of scrimmage. While running, the quarterback can easily initiate the ready position, passing position and passing action, as previously explained.

Passing Coaching Points

The following coaching points should be remembered when teaching any pass:

1. Get away from the center as quickly as possible.
2. Do not false step.
3. Look downfield immediately.
4. Get ready (the ready position) to pass quickly.
5. If setting up to throw, stand tall and straight.
6. Never lower the ball past the shoulder area.
7. Never wind up or bring the ball down, back, and around as if "pitching" it.
8. Keep the elbow above the shoulder on the pass.
9. Pass quickly when the receiver *begins* to get open.
10. Aim and throw at a target (helmet).
11. Follow through with the body.
12. Cover the pass after it is thrown.

If passing the ball on the run:

1. Do not jostle the ball while running.
2. Get to the proper depth and turn upfield.

3. A prominent error is to get too shallow to the line of scrimmage.
4. Square the shoulders (whether running left or right) to the line of scrimmage or the intended receiver.
5. "Run after the ball" once it is released.

2

Attacking Defenses with
Passing Strategy

There are many details to consider
when a pass offense is to attack any defense successfully. Since a football
field is large in area and teams can play on any portion, different strategical
aspects of the game must be thought of well in advance. Certain pass patterns
such as the long post or flag routes, for example, are good anywhere on the
field except near the goal line. These routes would have to be made shorter or
executed in another way. They may not even be called by the quarterback at
all. The same occurs with offensive formations. When a team is on the hash
mark there isn't enough field area to spread flankers and split ends into the
sideline, although there would be enough room to institute similar formations
on the wide side of the field. If a coach is to properly and strategically attack
to the fullest extent, he cannot do it with pass actions and patterns executed
haphazardly. Some pass routes may be good with the sprint-out pass but may
fail completely with dropback action. Tight or closed formations may be
excellent for play action passes or sprint-outs, but again, will not be successful with the dropback series. Some of the important segments of any successful passing attack that are not well planned in advance by some coaches will
be included within this chapter. They comprise formation variances, personnel, motion, shifting, field strategy and other ingredients that must blend well
with quarterback pass actions and receiver routes.

PERSONNEL

As previously mentioned, a coach must know the kind of quarterback
and receivers he has before any installation of a pass offense is introduced to

31

his team. If a quarterback is tall and slow, the dropback pass may be best. However, if he is fast and quick, but small, the sprint or roll-out may suit him better. What formation(s) a coach will utilize is an important factor. If a coach has two or three excellent split ends, he may want to utilize some form of a spread formation with no tight end alignment. However, if the coach has only one or two split ends, but a big and strong tight end, he may desire to install a tight end-split end concept with the formations he employs. As can be seen, personnel play a significant factor with any successful passing attack that not only includes the type of pass actions involved, but the formations to be used. The coach must evaluate the personnel he has available and make the best of what he has at hand.

FORMATION VARIANCES FOR ATTACK

Formations, as just stated, can be determined by the personnel. However, there are other strategical aspects that should be emphasized with the formations desired. They include the type of pass route preferred, the pass game wanted, and the defensive adjustments that occur for certain pass patterns to find success.

Strengths and Weaknesses of Formation Patterns*

Every coach should know the strengths and weaknesses of the formations he uses or prefers to add to his repertoire, so he can utilize them to their fullest extent. The following are a few formation variances a coach can utilize with the strengths and weaknesses included.

Line Variations

Tight End (Diagram 2-1)

The tight end is aligned in an excellent position to block at the off-tackle hole and execute double team blocking with his offensive tackle. He is in position to release on pass routes, although he could be held up on the line by a linebacker or defensive end. His routes will be determined by any offensive back stationed outside him.

Diagram 2-1

Nasty Tight End (Diagram 2-2)

The end is still in position to block for the off-tackle hole, but if the defense adjusts to show other looks, the blocking may not be as successful.

---

*For a fuller explanation of strengths and weaknesses of formations and their variations, refer to Drew Tallman, *How to Coach Football's Attacking Defenses* (West Nyack, N.Y.: Parker Publishing Co., 1973), pp. 47-66.

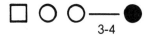

Diagram 2-2

However, he is in a better alignment to release for a pass inside or outside, and may not be held up on the line quite as easily.

Split End (Diagram 2-3)

The split end is in excellent position to release from the line of scrimmage either inside or outside for the pass game. The defense must widen to cover his alignment, which may be advantageous for some pass patterns. He can not block at the off-tackle hole, but maintains a width to angle inside and block defenders for any wide play.

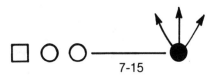

Diagram 2-3

Wing (Diagram 2-4)

The wingback is in a good spot to block for outside and off-tackle plays, and can reverse or counter back on certain play actions. He can release to the flat quickly. The tight end-wing combination is probably suited better for blocking purposes than for throwing the ball. Only a few pass patterns can be executed well from it, it does not widen the defense, and the sprint or roll-out pass action should only be executed.

Diagram 2-4

Nasty Wing (Diagram 2-5)

The wing split is about 4 to 5 yards. He is in a good location to help on any outside running play in collaboration with the tight end's assistance. The nasty wing alignment will widen the defensive halfback or corner slightly, which may be a benefit for certain pass routes.

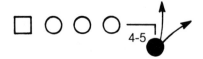

Diagram 2-5

Flanker (Diagram 2-6)

The flanker is an excellent formation for it widens the defensive corner, spreads the defense, and forces inside linebackers to cover wider and extended areas. Good pass combinations (width and two receivers) are the result. The flanker is similar to a split end and can release from the line both inside or outside. However, he is eliminated from the backfield for ball carrying responsibilities.

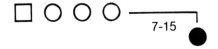

Diagram 2-6

Slot, Nasty Slot, Wide Slot (Diagram 2-7)

The slot, nasty slot, and wide slot are similar to the advantages and disadvantages of the wing, nasty wing, and flanker. However, many defensive schemes are not familar with the slot and nasty slot—therefore different blocking and pass routes can be accomplished. The wide slot is often seen, however, and the pass patterns which were successful with the flanker formation may not achieve similar accomplishments with the wide slot. The reasons are obvious. The wide slot can easily cause the defensive front (linebackers) to adjust off the line of scrimmage and, therefore, be in a better position to cover pass routes. Most definitely a coach must keep this in mind when attacking defenses from this offensive look.

Spread (Diagram 2-8)

The passing game advantage of the spread slot is that it offers two quick receivers that can release inside or outside from the line of scrimmage. It forces the defenders to spread on alignment. It compels the defensive linebackers to either align near the bulk of the formation or adjust outside. The offense can easily utilize either the passing routes or the running plays according to the linebackers' positions. This offensive alignment also offers the wide receivers the opportunity to block inside for an outside running play (options, power, etc.).

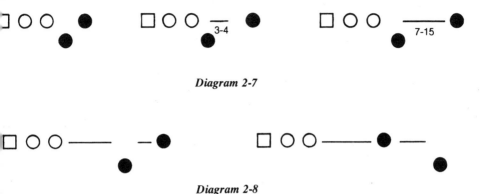

Diagram 2-7

Diagram 2-8

Backfield Variations

"I" Look (Diagram 2-9)

The "I" Formation focuses its use to more of the running game. The deep offensive back can run in either direction on power or the option game. However, the "I" is good for the sprint draw especially where width is included with the formation.

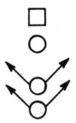

Diagram 2-9

Regular Backfield (Diagram 2-10)

The halfback is in a prime position to release on pass routes, regardless of whether he is set to the weak or strong portion of the offensive set. He is in a good running and diving location also.

Split Backs (Diagram 2-11)

This is the best passing backfield set because it positions two offensive backs in the backfield for the threat of the run, and at the same time they can release on pass routes or flare control assignments. Running plays in either

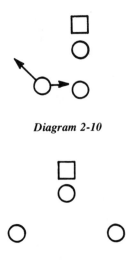

Diagram 2-10

Diagram 2-11

direction, cross-bucks, power and diving can be unfolded. Play action, boot-legs, and sprint-outs can be used as well.

Formations and Defensive Adjustments

When strategically attacking defenses with the passing game, it should be pointed out that certain offensive formations do better against some defenses and vice versa. For example, a spread formation with two split ends and a flanker may pass circles around a three deep defense because of the width the two defensive halfbacks and one safety must cover. A four deep defense, however, should be more successful because it can spread out, utilize rotation or invert, and blitz from man to man. While linebackers can be brought off from the line with a three deep, the same strategy can be accomplished with the four deep. Some defenses utilize only one or two linebackers while others may use three or four. The offensive set shown may determine the defense used, and therefore, certain strategical pass patterns can be unleashed versus it.

When an offense faces one particular defense, a similar concept holds true. As indicated in Diagram 2-12, a flanker formation is presented versus the Split-Four Defense. In this case, the only defender covering the flat and curl area is the defensive halfback. Diagram 2-13 illustrates a wide slot alignment versus the Split-Four defense. However, in this situation the defensive outside linebacker can easily adjust off the line into a better pass coverage position. The defense is in a preferable alignment, therefore, to cover the pass from the wide slot formation rather than from the flanker set. It is significant, therefore, to *know* and *understand* the formations called and the defensive

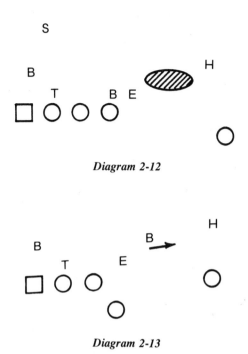

Diagram 2-12

Diagram 2-13

adjustments that can easily and automatically be utilized by the defense. In every case, the offense must take advantage of these adjustments, whether they will assist in the passing patterns, running phases of the passing game, or other running actions of the offense.

Formation and Pass Games

The formations used will, in many instances, formulate the type of pass game a coach utilizes. For example, with a tight or closed formation (wing-T, slot, split end, etc.), the sprint or roll out attack can be used. Play action passes work well also. With the sprint or roll-out pass game the quarterback is throwing to one side. Backs and ends can release toward the action and execute dependable routes for the quarterback to easily see and throw to. Three offensive backs are usually aligned in some fashion for the faking of running and counter plays. This tends to freeze linebackers and, in a few instances, the deep secondary. The receivers are already releasing when this is done and the quarterback is maneuvering with his play action fake to one side or the other before the pass is thrown.

The spread formations, such as the flanker-split end or wide slot situations, are geared predominantly for the dropback pass, although the sprint-out pass can operate also. Since width, depth, and various distances are available, different and divergent pass patterns can be developed to confuse the defense. The receivers are not assembled close together. Therefore, the linebackers and secondary can not cover or assist other teammates. As previously mentioned they must cover sizable areas of the field, which makes it even more difficult to make interceptions.

Formations and Pass Patterns

Any pass game can develop various pass patterns, but only some are effective with the type of formations adopted. For example, a tight end-wing situation is entirely different than a tight end-flanker set. A split end with a halfback in his regular position is more diversified than a wide spread (split end and flanker). Illustrated in Diagram 2-14 are three examples of a tight wing, flanker, and spread with the same pass pattern called. As can be seen, the defensive coverage and offensive receiver and quarterback timing are all entirely unrelated. Add on the width difference factor (flanker could be seven yards or he could stretch it to seventeen yards depending upon field position) with the pass action involved and the coach has an entirely different strategical look to aid in completing the pass.

Once a coach finally determines the offensive plan and formation he would like to use for his team, then pass patterns of various widths and depths should be developed. Splitting adjustments can be made with each offensive formation so the defensive change desired for the particular pattern will hopefully be made.

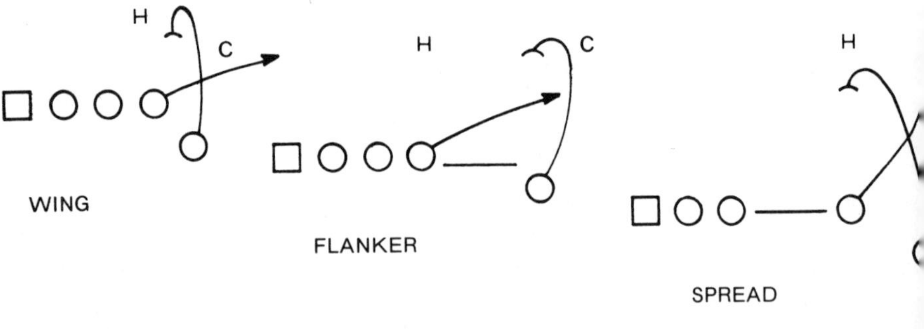

WING

FLANKER

SPREAD

Diagram 2-14

ATTACKING WITH MOTION

Motion is utilized to alter a formation after the original offensive set has been stationary for one second. The reasoning for motion is obvious. Depending upon the type of motion used, the defense can only react within the framework of seconds. In most instances, this will furnish the offense an advantage for two reasons. First, the defense must react to the changing formation and will not know when the ball is to be hiked. Therefore, an offensive back going in motion toward a tight end could be a wing, nasty wing or a flanker when the ball is snapped. Second, the defense may have to adjust its defensive pass coverage and scheme inside for both the passing and running phases. Motion can also assist passing to a back coming off the line of scrimmage. For example, if a back is aligned as a flanker, the defense can set up properly and use the "bump and run" concept. However, if the back is sent in motion in order to become a flanker, the defensive halfback can not cover him as closely and, therefore, the "bump and run" principle is eliminated.

Motion can improve the passing game of many offensive formations, and it may be used for the following five purposes:

1. To Create Strength
2. To Change Strength
3. To Create Balance
4. To Create Position
5. To Create Weakness

1. Creating Strength

Creating strength with a formation has many advantages. It can flood a particular area of the field, spread the defense with numerous routes, or it can put a linebacker on a man-to-man basis to cover an offensive back (a mismatch). Diagram 2-15 illustrates motion for strength in attacking defenses.

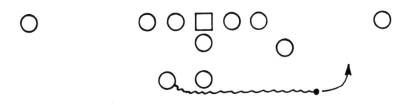

Diagram 2-15

2. Changing Strength

Changing offensive strength can have the defense adjust one way and compel it to readjust as motion is taking place. The defenders are now on the move, which may help free or create single coverage for some of the offensive receivers (Diagram 2-16).

3. Creating Balance

Situating strength on one side for defensive alignments and reverting back through motion to a balance set may also be helpful at times. Diagram 2-17 shows this aspect of motion.

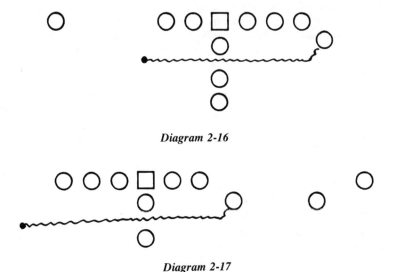

Diagram 2-16

Diagram 2-17

4. Creating Position

Diagram 2-18 indicates an offensive formation with quick motion. While this does not change formation balance, it can establish sudden pressure on the defense and can add different pass patterns that were not first expected.

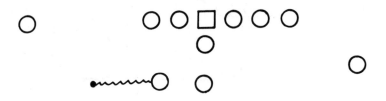

Diagram 2-18

5. Creating Weaknesses

Arranging a formation weak to a side is advantageous to any passing team. At times this can position a receiver away from motion, creating a one on one situation with a defensive halfback. Linebackers, or possibly a defensive free safety, may adjust their coverage toward the formation or strength. The receiver away from motion is availed of an excellent opportunity to execute various routes that normally would have been unsuccessful (Diagram 2-19).

A team can adopt numerous and varied styles of motion. They include

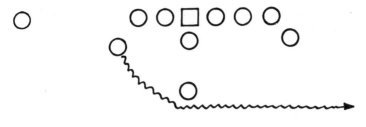

Diagram 2-19

short, medium, and long motion patterns, with action to or away from the formation. Whatever is utilized, however, there should be a *purpose* for it. The formation and motion designed must be integrated with the pattern used, the quarterback action from it, the defensive adjustment made, etc. Without planned strategical movement, there is absolutely no sense in employing it.

ATTACKING WITH SHIFTING

Many aspects in shifting from one formation to another can be beneficial. Shifting can be achieved by one or more offensive players moving to other alignments forming another formation. This can be advantageous to the particular play called. Since every player can shift, entire offensive formations can be changed, compelling a quick adjustment by the defense before the snap of the football. Of course, the offense must be set for at least one second before the ball is snapped. Similar to motion, shifting formations can change strengths, but also create position, balance, weaknesses and other strengths. Diagram 2-20 indicates a shift from a tight formation to a wide open offensive set. While the defense has the opportunity to adjust, it must react quickly to alignments, responsibilities, keys, coverages, etc.

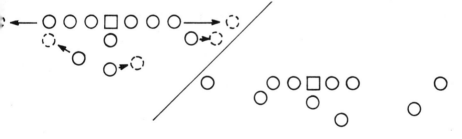

Diagram 2-20

SHIFTING AND MOTION FOR ATTACKING PURPOSES

When the offense can add both concepts of shifting and motion, it can create problems for the defense. If the offense utilizes the different personnel variances and proper play calling with strategical maneuvering, the defense may not be able to adjust properly. It may also have to stay in one defensive scheme. As a result, the offense can attack the defense both on the ground and in the air with greater ease, because it knows exactly what the defense is going to do.

SHIFTING, MOTION, AND AN UNBALANCED CONCEPT

While shifting and motion have already been explained, the offense can add balanced or unbalanced line concepts. The defense may never know what to expect, and at the same instance will have to react quickly in order to adjust properly. Diagram 2-21 illustrates shifting with motion forming an unbalanced line.

The reader may speculate that the combinations of shifting, motion, and unbalanced lines can cause some individual breakdowns or miscues from its players. This is NOT so. If a coach has a basic formula in calling formations, then it is quite easy to add the concepts of shift and/or motion. As long as there is a purpose of attack designed and planned, these concepts described become important. Shifting, motion, and unbalanced lines do not have to be installed to have a good passing attack. However, adding a few or some of the ideas presented can be, as mentioned, advantageous for the offense.

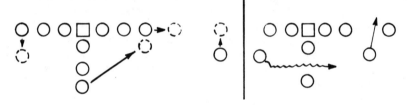

Diagram 2-21

ATTACKING WITH THE "MOVE"

An offensive formation can "move" one player to another position, and then hold him for a fraction of a second (less than one second as required with the shift) before the snap of the football. This is an important ingredient to any pass attack—i.e. the formation changes, certain passing strengths can develop, defenses have less than a second to react, and a defender may be out of position to cover various pass patterns. For an example of a "move," Diagram 2-22 illustrates an inside linebacker covering a deep tailback man-to-man. The tailback moves to the line of scrimmage. If the inside linebacker's reaction is slow or he is not prepared, the tailback has a strategical position and can jump off the line of scrimmage into the defensive area, and then should be clear on different pass routes.

ATTACKING WITH FIELD STRATEGY

Pass patterns, as mentioned previously, are contingent upon distinct widths along the line of scrimmage and in the backfield. Depth may become a

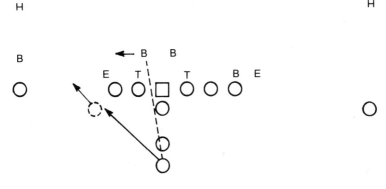

Diagram 2-22

factor in the backfield also. Many depth and width variations are subject to the location of the ball on the field. The length of the pattern (depth) will be controlled by the field also. Each formation, its variation and pattern called, therefore, must be initiated with the idea of where the ball is spotted. For example, if the ball is placed on the left hash mark, then a receiver stationed to the left only has 15 yards to adjust his split according to the route or pattern called. However, if he is positioned to the wide side of the field, he has approximately 32 yards to maneuver the split and execute routes. This becomes a significant aspect to any pass offense. Since there is a wide difference in the space available, only certain pass patterns or ideas of strategical attack can be used toward the sideline. However, almost all routes can be executed to the middle of the field.

Placing formations toward the sideline or toward the wide side of the field must be considered also. Sprint-outs, dropbacks, play action passes, bootlegs, and waggles play an important role in regard to field position. Diagram 2-23 clearly illustrates formations toward and away from the sidelines and how field areas can dictate the pass patterns called. With the formation set toward the sidelines, as shown, the defense has a better opportunity to cover pass routes by utilizing the sidelines as a "twelfth man." In other words, from a width standpoint the formation toward the wide side of the field has a better chance to attack the defense with success.

While it has been indicated that the formation was more viable to the wide side of the field, there are many instances where the formation set into the sideline is also enticing. If the offense can use proper field strategy in attacking the defenses encountered, more and more games can be won through these ideas and concepts. An example would be if a defensive secondary employing a Monster scheme rotated toward the wide side of the field. The offense could situate formations back toward the sidelines and attack the defense from there.

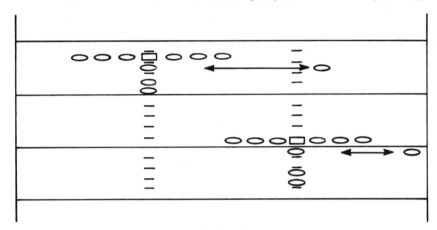

Diagram 2-23
***The same formation shown to the field
and sidelines***

If the football is spotted in the middle of the field, the offense can align its formation in either direction, or even spread it to both sides if a definite pass situation arises. As shown in Diagram 2-24, the offense has the ability to attack in either direction with the spacious width of the field.

Near the goal line, when the offense is driving for a score, some pass routes will either have to be adjusted or changed. The offense has only limited space to maneuver the routes and patterns called. Because of the field position, the defense does not have to cover large areas of the field. Therefore, the

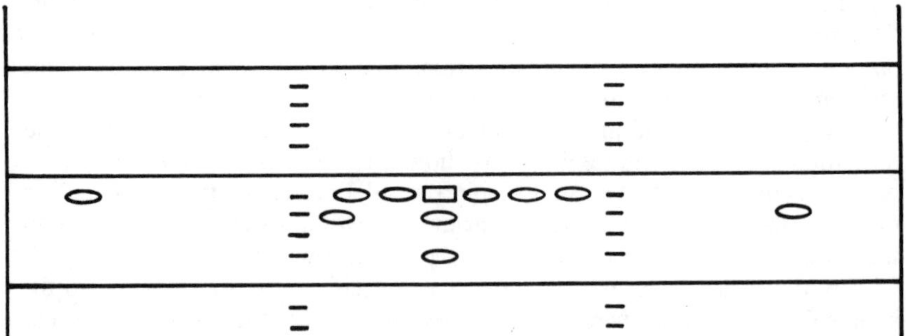

Diagram 2-24

goal line pass offense must be drilled and taught properly on both hashes and in the middle in order to strike with success. Also, routes must be called in this area to beat both the zone and man-to-man principles.

DOWN AND DISTANCE TENDENCIES

The pass game with formations can have a definite bearing on the down and distance situations. Some teams like to pass only when it is necessary (third and long), while others may throw 30 per cent of the time on any down. Some teams may pass regularly from 40 to 50 per cent of the time. Whatever the passing philosophy or statistics, it is *very important* to interpret the particular statistics and tendencies on all four downs correctly. The formation and down chart will indicate what the offense does on all downs from each formation. If the coach knows his own tendencies (through scouting and his own film observation), he will be prepared to fully change the statistics when defenses begin to adjust their schemes. The coach can now execute common pass plays on first and ten once done on third and long. Draws, screens, and shuffle passes can be replaced on the pass situation described also.

3

How to Attack Defensive

Pass Coverages

In order for any coach to effectively attack various pass defenses, it is imperative that a thorough knowledge of execution, responsibilities, variations, strengths and weaknesses of the coverages be comprehended. There is a substantial difference between a four spoke and three deep rotation and a four or three deep man-to-man. As the game approaches, the coach must know exactly what his opponent favors on various occasions, i.e., first and ten, third and long, second and short, etc. Through knowledgeable tendencies a coach will be better prepared for a strategical attack of the pass game.

There are a multitude of secondary coverages the pass game will encounter during a game and season. The zone coverage can be executed in various ways. There is the three deep, four spoke, two deep, rotation, invert, revert, etc. There are diverse man-to-man coverages, including man-to-man with blitzes, man coverage with no stunts, and man-to-man with one or two free safeties. At the same time, there are a combination of zone coverages on one side of the field and/or formation, with man-to-man executed on the other. Stunting can be done with this concept also. With these different coverages, how does a coach go about attacking each one? There are different methods to accomplish this which, as will be seen, are rather simple.

METHODS OF ATTACKING ALL PASS DEFENSES

A few coaches desire a method of practicing pass patterns, but also have a system where others could be formulated during a game. This may sound somewhat haphazard, but if planned ahead for unexpected defensive situations, a particular pattern may be necessary versus the coverage used.

Another method is to plan offensive pass patterns that will be successful versus almost any secondary coverage. This includes man-to-man and zone. There are numerous patterns to be considered in this matter. Of course, timing between the quarterback and receivers becomes a significant factor because open areas will be totally incomparable when executed versus zone and then man-to-man.

Some coaches want quarterbacks to "read" secondary coverages. This can be accomplished before and/or after the snap of the football. There is a wide variation in the degree of reading coverages. Some coaches require reading only with the wide receivers or possibly the second receiver inside (tight end, slot back). Other coaches desire the offensive backs to read both on flare control and organized patterns. A few teams want to establish a highly organized and efficient method of reading with the quarterback, backs and all receivers. This is a very sophisticated attack to accomplish, and substantial time is necessary within the practice schedule in order for success to occur.

Whatever the kind of pass offense installed, it is important for the coach to have a well thought out plan and organization of how patterns and routes are to be taught, drilled, and understood. The strategy of attack, no matter what offense is employed, must have at least the opportunity to succeed. Haphazardly calling patterns just will not work.

ATTACK ONE PORTION OF THE FIELD

When attacking pass defenses, a quarterback should be cognizant of the fact that calling a pass pattern to one side or area of the field is easier than concentrating on the entire field from sideline to sideline. As the ball is snapped the quarterback can now see the defensive adjustments, reactions and coverages easily to the one section only. If the particular pattern is covered and the quarterback cannot release the football, then he can pick out his alternate receivers or routes. This should not be culminated, however, until all possibilities of the particular pattern are fulfilled.

THE CONCEPTS OF PASS DEFENSES

Every pass coverage has a fundamental principle in order for it to be successful. Concepts and techniques of pass defenses are different and each will be described.

Zone Defense

The zone pass defense covers various areas of the field. Each defender is responsible for his particular part and will only assist his teammate when the ball is in the air. Different zones and responsibilities are mapped out on the field for the defenders. These zones may alter from play to play according to the action of-the football. When the pass is indicated, the defenders attempt to get as much depth as necessary. The secondary doesn't allow anyone behind them, and containment of the pattern is desired. Linebackers sprint to their areas and cover underneath the defensive halfbacks. These areas and patterns include the flat, hook, curl, middle, etc. With some actions of the quarterback, a few areas of the field are left uncovered. However, the defense can eliminate them because of the relationship of the passer to those particular areas and receivers. Once the ball is in the air, all the defenders will sprint to the football, hoping to gain an interception or at least throw a block if an interception is made.

Man-to-Man Defense

One defender is responsible for an offensive receiver with man-to-man coverages. No matter where the receiver progresses (unless the play dictates otherwise), the defender will stay with him. Some man-to-man secondary coverages utilize blitzes, which can assist the defenders because the time element becomes essential. The less time the quarterback has to throw the ball, the less time the defender has to cover the receiver. In other instances, when one or two free safeties are used, the man-to-man defender is covered behind him. If the receiver overruns him long, the free defensive halfback or safety will assist on the coverage.

Strengths and Weaknesses of Zone Defense

The strengths of the zone pass defense are as follows:

1. Each defender is responsible for one area alone. Speed is not necessary if a particular receiver is fast.
2. Reaction to the ball only comes once the ball is in the air.
3. When the ball is in the air all defenders are going after it. If taught properly, all defenders should be keeping their eyes on the passer.
4. The long pass is well covered, since the main responsibilities of the defensive halfbacks and safeties are to stay as deep as the deepest receivers.
5. There are always defenders in position to cover other phases of the passing game, such as draws, screens, etc.
6. Defenders are not run out of position, so if the quarterback decides to run with the football, the defense is prepared to come up and tackle him.
7. It can be taught easily, for it is relatively simple for players to learn and understand.

The weaknesses of the zone coverages are as follows:

1. There are many seams or vacated areas that result within the secondary. If the receivers can proceed to the open seams, passes can easily be completed.
2. Not all zones can be covered on the field at one time. If they are, there isn't a good rush being established on the quarterback.
3. Flooding receivers into one zone or area places tremendous pressure on one defender.
4. There are vacated areas in front and in back of linebackers, and in front of defensive halfbacks.

5. More of an area, from both a width and depth standpoint, must be covered by the defense if the quarterback has the time to throw the ball.

6. If a rush is necessary, and a zone coverage is used, there will be many vacated areas when various linebackers stunt.

ATTACKING ZONE COVERAGES

There are basically three deep zone coverages being used extensively in football today. They include the two deep, three deep and four deep looks.

Two Deep Zone Coverage

The two deep zone coverage is being accomplished from the three and four spoke secondaries in one way or another. When complete zone is used, there will be four, five, or even six defenders positioned for the underneath coverage. Diagram 3-1 indicates the two deep zone coverage with weakness areas shown.

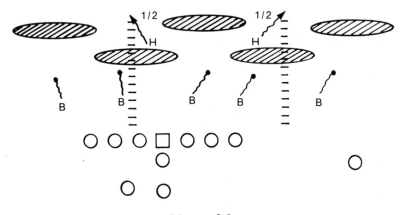

Diagram 3-1

Attack—Since there are only two defenders operating in the deep zones, the weaknesses are located there. The offense can treat the two deep zone as if it were a three deep rotation. Three to four receivers should release deep, forcing a two on four relationship (Diagram 3-2). The offense should attempt to exploit the deep outside weakness areas near the sideline above the flat. This can be underneath the defensive halfback as well (Diagram 3-3). A receiver may have to be sent into the flat to "hold" the defender responsible for the area. If good depth is not being achieved by the linebackers, then the offense can attack underneath the defensive halfback beyond the linebackers. Attempting to hit the seam areas between linebackers is also a good idea.

Three Deep Zone Coverage

The three deep zone coverage adds another defender to the defensive secondary, as indicated in Diagram 3-4. A team can align in the three deep

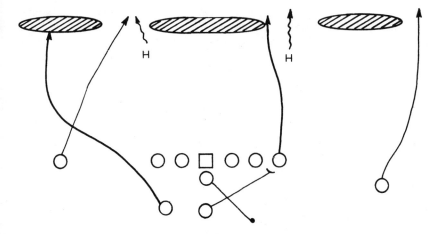

Diagram 3-2

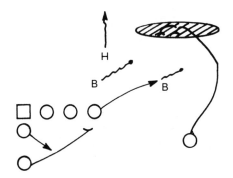

Diagram 3-3

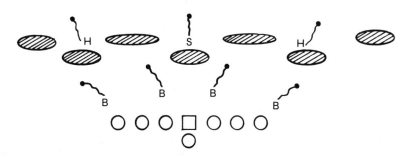

Diagram 3-4

positions or can revolve easily to it. Many defensive schemes possess three secondary defenders directly (Split-4, Wide Tackle-6, 5-3, etc.), utilize a "Monster" effect, or rotate from the nine man front defenses (5-4, Pro-4, Eagle-5, etc.). In most cases, four linebackers are positioned to cover the underneath areas in one fashion or another. This is relative, of course, to the defense used and the quarterback's actions.

Attack—Since there is an added defender, as described with the two deep, there is less area or open space for attack. When passing long, two offensive receivers can be routed to one area versus a defender. Directing a four on three ratio of receivers to defenders can be done also. If the linebackers do not attain depth, open areas can result in front of the defensive halfbacks and safety. A substantial weakness occurs in the underneath coverage. If the basic four man rush is employed, there are only four defenders underneath responsible for such areas as flat zones, hook zones, curl areas and the middle portion of the field. In many cases, the outside linebacker (or end dropping off) has a difficult assignment in covering the flat and curl areas, especially if offensive width is accompanied with the formation.

Another disadvantage to the three deep is a two wide-out formation (flanker-split end). This can stretch the three deep across the field, causing some burdens both deep and short. Inside linebackers find it difficult to cover the curl positions. Establishing a three man flood pattern to one side of the field (causing a three on two relationship with the two linebackers) constitutes an excellent choice versus this alignment (Diagram 3-5).

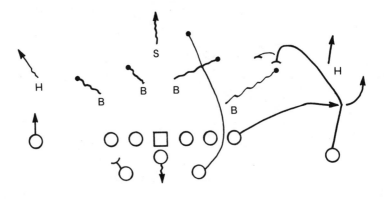

Diagram 3-5

Four Deep Zone Coverage

The four spoked zone coverage is not utilized often, since the secondary defenders are assigned to the deep ¼ portions of the field (Diagram 3-6).

Attack—It is difficult to attack this secondary long because of the four defenders. However, three linebackers can only be used underneath, unless a defender is removed from the rush. The offense should attack this scheme

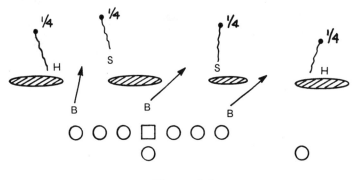

Diagram 3-6

underneath between the seams, over and under the linebackers, and with the thought of flooding an area with two or three receivers versus one defender.

Rotation Coverage—Three Deep

A rotational three deep secondary is used extensively by a number of defenses. If the flow of the football is toward the formation, the defensive halfback will rotate forward and be responsible for the flat, and the single safety covers the outside 1/3 of the field. This can be done with the dropback attack as well. The offside defensive halfback is assigned to the remaining 2/3's of the deep secondary. The strength of this movement lies in the fact that an eight man defensive front is employed versus the offense and another defender is assigned in the flat. This can free a linebacker for a rush also. Of course, weaknesses of the coverage exist, and they are shown in Diagram 3-7.

Attack—When rotation occurs, natural weaknesses result in the deep secondary. The offense should attack the rotation as if it were the two deep look. It is pointed out, however, that the defensive safety and halfback are

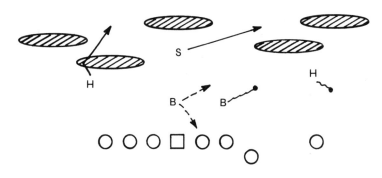

Diagram 3-7

reacting to their responsibilities, even though they are not aligned in them. Therefore, sizable deficiencies occur within this aspect of the coverage.

The deep outside 1/3 of the field should be attacked with various pass routes and patterns. Square-outs and hooks can be used with success. The basic sprint-out pass can be successful, as shown in Diagram 3-8. The wing-back "holds" the defensive halfback in the flat, while the tight end sprints at an angle behind him. He can stay on a straight course or turn outside. Releasing three or four receivers deep or sending two receivers versus one and dividing the area are good choices. Routing a receiver toward the defensive safety's original position can also be successful.

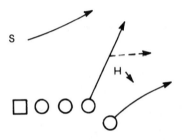

Diagram 3-8

The designed throwback pass from sprint-out action adds another dimension for strategical attack. With rotation, all the strength of the defense is geared in that direction. If the offense can sprint-out forcing automatic rotation and then pull up to throwback, open areas should result. Rolling the quarterback in one direction, forcing rotation (Diagram 3-9), and reversing

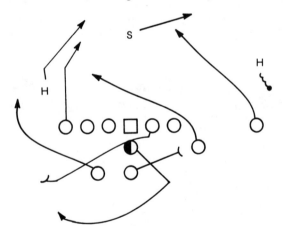

Diagram 3-9

back the opposite way is a good method of attacking rotation coverage. As previously stated, attacking the seam areas and different depth positions versus zone should be effective.

Rotational Coverage—Four Deep

The four spoke rotational coverage has more strength in the secondary because of the four defenders. The secondary can rotate in either direction, always resulting in a three deep defense, with the flat toward the rotation being accounted for. The defensive corner (H) is responsible for the flat, while the strong safety rotates to the outside 1/3 and the offside safety covers the middle 1/3. The away defensive cornerback (H) drops back to the offside outside 1/3 of the field. Rotation is often used with closed or tight offensive formations, although it can be employed versus any set. Diagram 3-10 illustrates the four deep rotation with weakness areas included.

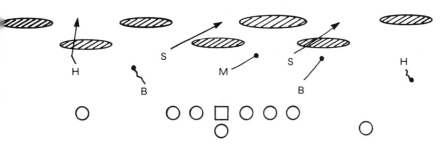

Diagram 3-10

Attack—The offense should attack the weakness areas whether they occur between defenders or in front of them. Passing diagonal routes opposite the rotation is good. If rotation is used on wide-out formations, the offense should attack the deep outside 1/3 toward it. Another weakness is the curl area between the rotating corner and outside linebacker attempting to cover that position. Other plays designed are the throwback pass, rolling in one direction and reversing back, and plays taking advantage of the underneath linebackers both inside and the flat area away from the rotation, since only three linebackers are usually involved with the four spoke secondary. Attacking with a two wide-out formation is best since the defenders have to extend (opening up areas) to cover their responsibilities.

Invert Coverage—Three Deep

Invert coverage from the three deep is not used extensively by many teams. When it is, however, it is usually employed versus tight or closed formations. If it is tried versus wide-out formations, the defensive safety will most likely cover the curl area with the flat either being unoccupied or an outside linebacker assigned to it. The strength lies in the deep outside 1/3 of the field and the curl zone. The coverage and weakness areas are indicated in Diagram 3-11.

Attack—The offense should immediately attack the defensive flat area if linebackers are not positioned there. Passing the ball long is excellent, especially within the weakness areas indicated. The deep outside may be well covered, but the seam between both defensive halfbacks can be attacked. A simple post route (Diagram 3-12) either thrown long or beyond the defensive safety's responsibility is good. Since the backside is essentially the same as the rotated three deep, the offense should accomplish similar strategies toward it.

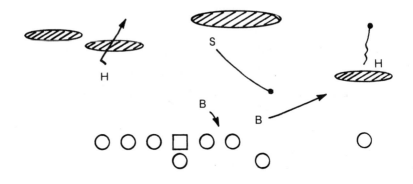

Diagram 3-11

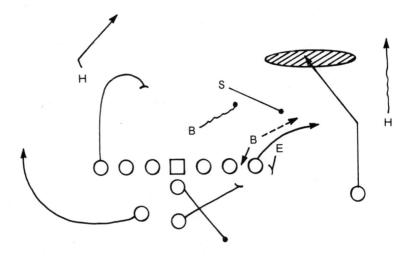

Diagram 3-12

Invert Coverage—Four Deep

The only difference between the invert zone coverage and rotation is that the defensive halfback and safety toward the flow switch assignments. The defensive halfback converges through the deep outside 1/3 of the field, while the safety "inverts" forward to secure the flat area. The strength of the coverage is the deep outside 1/3, which is covered immediately. Also, the flat-curl area is accountable, especially versus wide-out formations. The defense still produces a three deep nucleus with one defender assigned to the flat (Diagram 3-13).

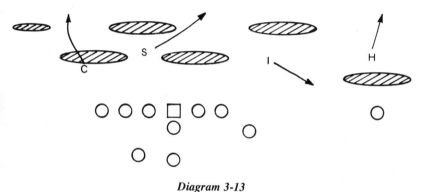

Diagram 3-13

Attack—The weak areas resulting from the invert zone four spoke are the outside flat areas (quick outs or hitch-hooks) and the area vacated by the original alignment of the invert defender. The offense should attack these areas as much as possible and also the seams between the defensive halfbacks and safeties. A weakness can develop in the deep middle if the offense can force the invert safety to take a course through the middle. This is especially advantageous when inverts are aligned on both sides of the offensive set. In some cases, the receivers can stun an invert man in this situation, because the defender may have his back to him. Spreading offensive formations may also be beneficial versus the four deep inverts. Diagram 3-14 illustrates two simplified post patterns from a spread formation versus the invert coverage.

ATTACKING MAN-TO-MAN COVERAGES

Strengths and Weaknesses of Man-to-Man

The strengths of the man-to-man pass defense are as follows:

1. One defender is responsible for one receiver. When the defender is quicker and faster than the receiver, the defense gains the advantage.
2. Man-to-man defense allows additional stunting and blitzing without relinquishing any open areas of the field.

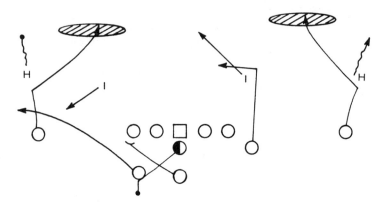

Diagram 3-14

The weaknesses of man-to-man pass defense are as follows:

1. If the offensive receiver is very talented, the offense has the advantage.
2. Once a secondary man makes a mistake (falls down or trips), there are no other defenders to assist him.
3. The route to be executed is well known to the receiver, while each defender must "read" the route on the run.

Man-to-Man—Three and Four Deep

When three deep man coverage is used, one or two linebackers are a necessity to cover other receivers out of the backfield. While stunting and blitzing can be done, other defenders must be responsible for all receivers. Since linebackers are not as quick and agile to cover them, especially offensive backs, the three deep becomes the weakest man-to-man pass defense. The four spoke, however, has an extra secondary man keying a receiver. He can become free if his assignment does not release on a route. Diagrams 3-15 and 3-16 illustrate the three and four deep man-to-man coverages.

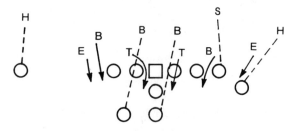

Diagram 3-15
The Split-4 Defense

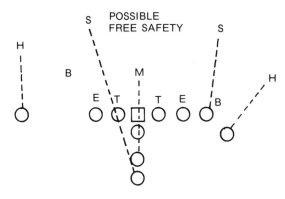

Diagram 3-16
The Pro-4 Defense

Attack—There are a number of methods of attacking man-to-man defenses. Following are some of the ways that can be used versus man-to-man concepts.

1. *Isolating a Receiver*—Isolating a receiver on a defender can easily be accomplished. Certain offensive formations can dictate this to a few defenses. An example is the flanker-split end set versus the three deep. The split end is automatically isolated against the one defensive halfback. Versus a four spoke, however, the offense would have to release the offensive backs. This, therefore, forces defenders to cover them in order to halt possible double coverage of a receiver. Flare control from the dropback offense is another example versus the four spoke. If the offensive back releases to the side of the potential free safety, the safety must pick him up. This, therefore, isolates the split end with the outside defensive halfback. Motion causes the secondary to adjust in another way. Diagram 3-17 indicates a safety being forced to take the offensive back, and Diagram 3-18 indicates motion effecting isolation.

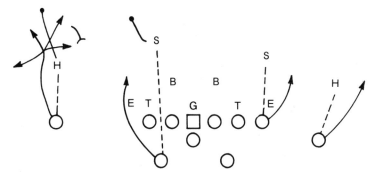

Diagram 3-17
The Split End can no longer be double covered.

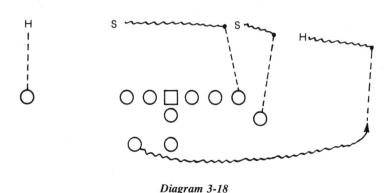

Diagram 3-18

Isolation does become important for when the offense has an excellent receiver, they can take advantage of this strength. The offensive receiver has a better opportunity to become free or open, and the pass has an improved percentage of completion.

2. *Forcing Linebackers to Cover Receivers*—The offense can compel linebackers to be responsible for receivers easily. For example, versus the three deep man-to-man, two receivers can release to the formation's offside, forcing automatic linebacker coverage. Three receivers can be directed to the strong side against the three or four spoke, while three receivers can be released weakside versus a four deep secondary. To simplifiy it, the offense can release five receivers versus the four spoke, and at least four receivers against the three deep. Diagram 3-19 illustrates one of many examples of compelling a linebacker to cover a potentially dangerous running back receiver.

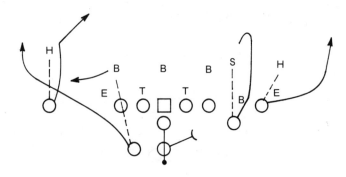

Diagram 3-19

3. *Executing Action Routes*—When a receiver is covered by a defender man-to-man, it is important that the executed routes do not decelerate, lag, or completely halt. Man-to-man secondaries can easily cover this type of route,

i.e., curl, hook, hitch, etc. Quick and accelerated routes should be used that make it difficult for a defender to overtake. Such routes include cross field, diagonal, square in, square out, post, flag, slant, etc. The longer the receiver is at an accelerated pace, the more difficult it becomes for the defender to stay with him.

4. *Pick Passes*—A pick pass involves at least two receivers on a pattern. One receiver executes a route that helps screen a defender as the other receiver scoots in the opposite direction. Diagram 3-20 illustrates the split end releasing from the line and running a short post route, as the slot back starts upfield but cuts outside. Many other patterns and formations could be developed also.

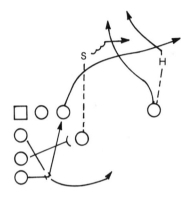

Diagram 3-20

5. *Play Action Passes*—Play action passes are good versus any man-to-man coverage. Faking ball carriers tend to freeze linebackers, and may cause many man-to-man defenders to come up quickly for the tackle. If the defensive halfback's key or read simulates a running block, the more reason he will go for the fake. As the defender advances forward for the tackle, the offensive receiver faking the block should release to his designated areas for the pass.

6. *Quarterback as a Receiver*—Another unexpected method to attack man-to-man coverages is the utilization of the quarterback. In most instances, he is not considered a threat as a receiver. An example of this pass is indicated in Diagram 3-21. The offensive halfback receives a pitch from the quarterback as if he were proceeding to run with the football. The halfback, however, pulls up behind his tackle's position and passes a cross continental back to the quarterback.

7. *Tackle Eligible Pass*—While the tackle eligible pass is outlawed in the college ranks, it can be an element of surprise against man-to-man. Actually, colleges could adopt it as long as the end man on the line of scrimmage has a number higher than seventy-nine. The split end must step back from the line in order to make the "tackle" eligible. The flanker on the side of the formation will step forward into the line. The tight end, in this situation, is not

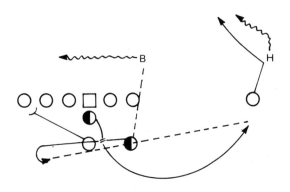

Diagram 3-21

eligible for a pass. Since a defender is not covering the tackle, he is usually free for the pass (Diagram 3-22).

    8. *Head and Shoulder Fakes*—Versus man-to-man coverages the receivers should use more head and shoulder fakes, since this can help in getting free. Forcing the defensive halfback to turn his body in one direction, and then pivoting away from him, is most effective.

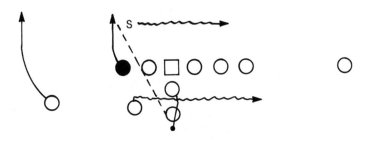

Diagram 3-22

ATTACKING MAN-TO-MAN—FREE SAFETIES

    There are various free safety defenses. Some utilize one free safety toward the back side of the formation. Another method is to set a free safety on the frontside or strength of the offensive formation. A third alternative is to position two free safeties with complete man-to-man underneath coverage. In all of these situations, offensive attack remains similar.

One Free Safety

    A free safety assists any man-to-man defense considerably. The defenders aligned on the side of the free safety can play tighter and more aggressive on the receiver(s). Diagram 3-23 illustrates one free safety situation.

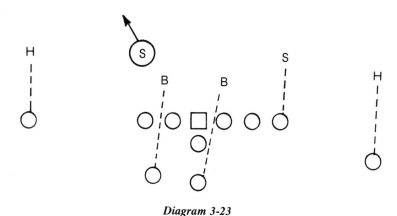

Diagram 3-23

Attack—With the safety located backside, the offense should attack the frontside of the defense as a complete man-to-man situation. On the backside where the free safety is aligned, the receiver routes and patterns should be altered. All man-to-man attack principles are employed, except the routes should not be geared deep. If depth is necessary, however, it should be thrown away from the free safety. Routes that can be run toward it include the square in, square out, cross field, drag patterns, possible delays, etc.

Two Free Safeties

A defense with two free safeties allows the linebackers and other personnel to play tough and aggressive on their offensive counterparts. Yet if they are overrun deep, they will be protected with the free safeties. Five defenders are necessary for man-to-man coverage underneath, and two safeties are aligned behind, as shown with the 5-4 Defense in Diagram 3-24.

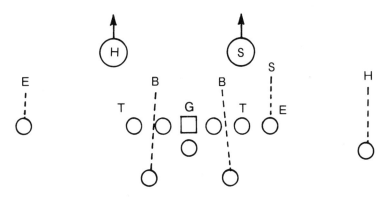

Diagram 3-24

Attack—Attacking this secondary coverage is similar to the one free safety. Shorter routes and patterns are preferable. Action routes are necessary in order to run away from the tough man-to-man techniques employed. Diagram 3-25 indicates a successful pass versus the two free safety situation. Two receivers are directed deep. This, therefore, delegates four defensive players to be responsible for both of them. While moving upfield, the outside receivers delay slightly and slant across the field. Usually one of these, flanker or split end, becomes free. Many other routes can be developed and expanded with success also.

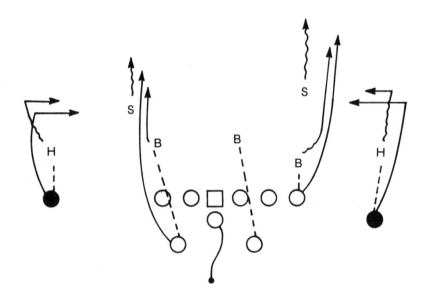

Diagram 3-25

ATTACKING ½ COVERAGES

Half coverage derives its name because half the secondary is using some segment of zone coverage, while the other half employs man-to-man principles. This coverage division is beneficial because zone principles can be utilized to the strong side of the formation. However, more importantly, if the offensive formation is meant to spread the defense and, therefore, the zones as well, it cannot do so because man-to-man is utilized. This coverage is excellent for three deep zone rotation because of the amount (three) of deep defenders. Diagram 3-26 illustrates half coverage.

Attack—Offensive attack of the secondary is rather easy since routes and patterns designed for zone coverage should be used to the zone side. Conversely, the man-to-man patterns should be utilized toward the man-to-man side.

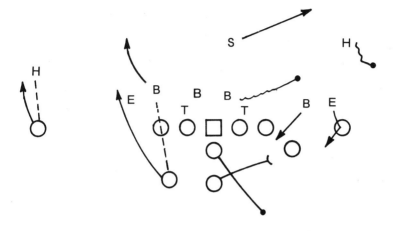

Diagram 3-26

4

Attacking the Underneath
Coverages

Defensive underneath coverages can
be geared toward simplicity or can be made complex. Many factors are
involved which depend upon the personnel utilized and the defense called.
While there are a multiple of defenses, each one has various adjustments,
stunts and blitzes. Not only does each defense change the assignments and
responsibilities of positions, but they alter the entire look, purpose, and
coverage of it. Linebackers are usually considered the underneath pass coverage of any defense. However, defensive ends can easily drop away from the
line at the snap of the ball on certain quarterback actions (Dropback, Sprint-
out Away) and assist in the defensive pass coverage. Secondary personnel can
rotate forward also. For any good pass offense to be successful, the underneath areas (including flat, hook, curl, middle) must be attacked with an
organized, systematic and, in some cases, imaginative plan. This chapter,
therefore, will present various ideas and ways to attack the underneath coverages of pass defenses in this manner.

Attacking Alignment

As previously stated, every defense will have various linebackers and/or
ends responsible for the underneath coverage. In most defensive schemes,
there will be three secondary defenders deep and four men underneath them.
Rotation of the four spoke secondary will bring a defensive halfback into the
flat. Three other defenders, therefore, are needed short. The three deep defense does not have to rotate or invert and, therefore, four defenders from the
forcing unit must be used.

The offense should exploit the alignment by attacking linebacker and underneath coverage. As an example, there is a great deal of difference in the abilities of the defenses to control the curl area. The Pro-4 Defense can direct their outside linebacker to that location, whereas the 5-4 defense must utilize their inside linebacker (Diagram 4-1). This becomes an important factor in attacking the curl area. Other examples could be readily shown also. Since weakness areas are indicated on alignment alone, the quarterback and coach can already pick and exploit the strengths and weaknesses of the defenses and variations involved. When weaknesses are clearly known, the offense has a better opportunity to attack each one and gain better results from it.

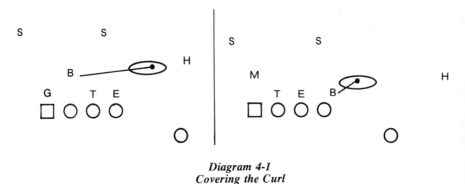

Diagram 4-1
Covering the Curl

The number of defenders adopted for underneath coverage is important also. For example, the 5-3 Odd-Diamond Defense has three linebackers available. If the defense devotes only those three linebackers underneath, then wider vacated areas develop for the offense to attack. The 5-4 Oklahoma defense may use two inside linebackers and a rotated halfback for underneath responsibilities. If another defender is desired, however, some teams drop off a defensive end. These various defenses and adjustments by different opponents become an important aspect of the passing game's strategical attack. When the alignment of the defense and the amount of defenders are known in advance, the offense has a better opportunity to complete passes, cut down interceptions and gain good yardage.

ATTACKING COVERAGES

Zone Underneath Coverage

When zone principles are applied, the offense should exercise routes and patterns that are likely to get receivers open between defenders (seam) and/or in front of or beyond them. The total number of defenders operating on certain pass actions should be known. This can be established and recognized well before or during a game. Is the defensive scheme mobilizing all the linebackers in the pass coverage, or are one or two blitzing across the line of scrimmage for the passer? Once this is discovered or realized, the offense can analyze the information and put it to good use. Diagram 4-2 illustrates one example of zone coverage with the receivers driving for the open seams. The same pass is indicated, in Diagram 4-2a, with a linebacker blitzing on flow and a wider area automatically developing in the coverage.

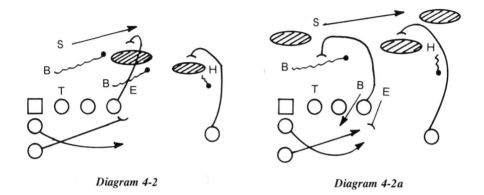

Diagram 4-2   Diagram 4-2a

Excellent choices of passes are ones that go beyond the linebacker coverage, but in front of the secondary. This is especially advantageous when the linebackers are not gaining proper depth, or the secondary is driven deep by another receiver (Diagram 4-3). The offense should attack linebackers by running receivers in front of them. This is especially beneficial when linebacker depth exceeds the normal. This may be due to the offensive receivers' longer patterns, forcing a deeper drop by the linebacker. Delay patterns should also be used when this occurs. Diagram 4-4 illustrates a delay halfback releasing from the backfield after the linebackers have gained depth.

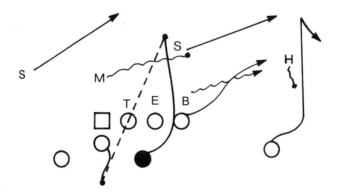

Diagram 4-3

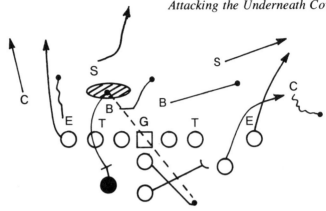

Diagram 4-4

The best pass routes versus zone underneath coverage are ones that will take place between the defenders. Such patterns include the hook, curl, and hitch. The square-out, square-in, and slant are others that will halt or decelerate into vacated areas. Flooding an area with more receivers than defenders should be tried. This can be a two on one or a three versus two situation.

Man-to-Man Underneath Coverage

When defensive man-to-man principles are practiced, other methods of attack must be accomplished. Attacking the man-to-man defenses, as described previously, should be accomplished. Receivers should not idle, decelerate, or stop, but should continue their routes in order to outrun the defender. The better pass patterns to execute are the square-in, square-out, post, flag, drag, cross, etc. Diagram 4-5 illustrates a short or medium pattern versus man-to-man coverage. Whether there is a free safety or not, these routes can be applied. Another excellent technique is the crossing of two or more receivers, hoping the defenders will bump and not have the opportunity to stay with their men.

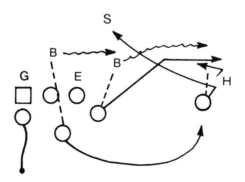

Diagram 4-5

PLAY ACTION PASSES

Play action passes are a favorable attacking device versus linebacker coverage. Defensive linebackers must respect a faking ball carrier driving into the line, which tends to hold or freeze them until they react to the quarterback rolling outside with the ball. The offense maintains an early advantage because the wide receivers can release easily from the line as if blocking downfield, while the inside receivers can fake a block for one or two counts before releasing. Therefore, receivers who have the quick and deceptive start should be able to get open early in the vacated areas.

Play action passes can be adopted from almost any type of play and/or series. Various routes and patterns can be used on each action pass as well. Diagram 4-6 indicates a tailback off-tackle play versus the 5-4 Defense, while Diagram 4-7 illustrates a play action pass from a quick hitting play. In every case the defensive linebackers must react forward or hold their ground until the pass is shown.

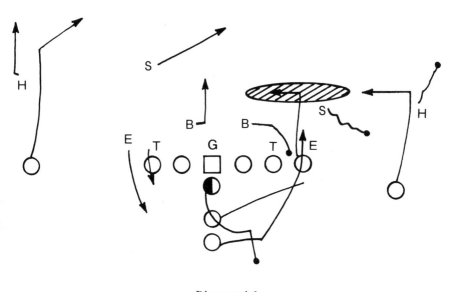

Diagram 4-6

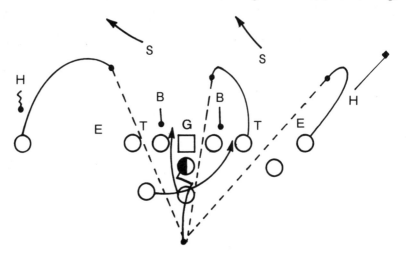

Diagram 4-7

ATTACK LINEBACKER REACTIONS

In most instances, linebackers enjoy the luxury of maneuvering quickly along the line of scrimmage, avoiding blocks because of their depth alignment. When they react or pursue quickly, the offense should have plays at their disposal to attack such situations. One idea is for a receiver to be quickly routed to an area the linebacker vacates. Diagram 4-8 illustrates a wishbone offense taking advantage of a rapidly pursuing linebacker from the 5-4 Defense. The quarterback steps out to mesh with the fullback on the split end

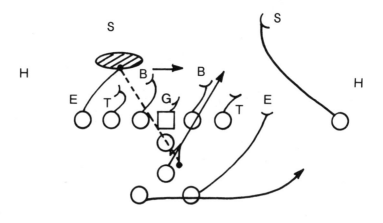

Diagram 4-8

side. The tight end releases from the line and immediately looks inside for the pass. The quarterback steps away from the fullback and releases the ball to him. Many examples from other play sequences can be developed also.

FLARE CONTROL

The dropback series and some sprint or roll-outs exploit flare control on linebackers. While the flare control principle is explained in detail in Chapter 7, it should be mentioned briefly here since it has the ability to control a linebacker for particular patterns. In some cases, a receiver may become open because the linebackers are not conscious of him.

The offensive back is responsible for a linebacker to his side. If the linebacker stunts or blitzes, the back assigned to him is responsible to block him. A few areas or routes will open up in the defensive secondary because of this rush. If a stunt does not occur, the offensive back can now be released on a preconceived route. This will force linebackers to cover him, which in effect controls their movement. For an example, a short or medium pattern is illustrated from a wide slot formation (Diagram 4-9). The split end executes a curl while the slot back releases toward the flat. The halfback keys the inside linebacker from the 5-4 defense and runs an inside pattern driving upfield, as shown. If the inside linebacker covers the flare back, the curl route should be open. If, however, the linebacker overruns the flare man to get to the curl position, the flare back is free. The quarterback should scan the field from outside-in and select the open receiver. Flare control routes can be instituted into all patterns, whether toward or away from the formation.

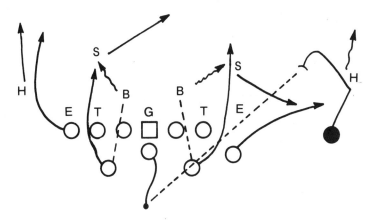

Diagram 4-9

DELAY ROUTES

Delay routes can be useful with all receivers. If the linebackers are playing zone, the delay receiver can wait until the linebackers gain depth before falling underneath them. When man-to-man coverage is shown, the defenders usually drop away as in zone, or may even disregard their man. When this occurs, receivers can become free. Diagram 4-10 illustrates a delay pattern versus the Pro-4 zone defense. The offensive flanker and halfback release from the line and attempt to drive the linebackers as deep as possible. The tight end sets as if to pass block. After approximately two counts, he releases over the vacated middle area. Timing is essential for this type of play, since the quarterback should have time to pass and the receivers must drive the linebacker as deep as possible. Numerous other delay tactics can also be achieved with the offensive backs and wide receivers.

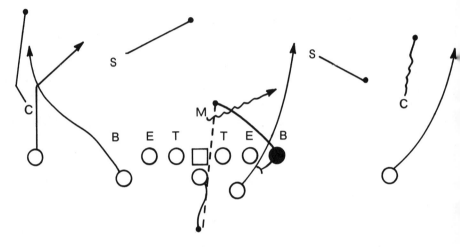

Diagram 4-10

READING LINEBACKER BLITZES

Defensive reading is discussed substantially in Chapter 6. However, some teams will pass the football on defensive reactions when linebackers stunt or blitz. A pass can be directed toward either side of the offensive formation (strong or weak) to a tight receiver or an offensive back. Flare control principles are used, but the offensive back never blocks. He automatically releases from his position, and as the linebacker stunts into the line he will look for and expect a pass from the quarterback. If a blitz does not occur, the flare control back or end is automatically into the designed pass pattern. Diagram 4-11 illustrates two examples of linebackers stunting, with the tight end and weakside halfback receiving the football from the reading quarterback.

DRAW PLAYS

The draw, which is the running phase of the passing game, can be an excellent weapon versus quick dropping linebackers. It can be good versus the stunting game as long as it can be blocked effectively. Draw plays can be

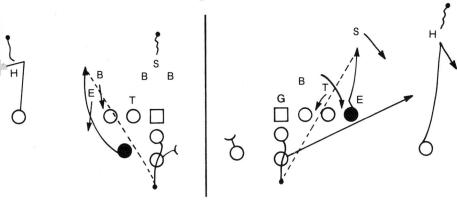

Diagram 4-11

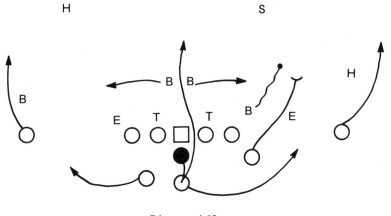

Diagram 4-12
The Quarterback Draw

adapted to all passing actions, including dropback, sprint-out and roll-out. An excellent draw play versus man-to-man underneath coverage is indicated in Diagram 4-12. The two offensive halfbacks release outside, forcing the defenders to cover them. The quarterback initiates three drop steps, indicating dropback action, but then springs upfield where the linebackers vacated. The sprint-out draw is another superb play. The quarterback sprints out toward his wide receivers. The linebackers must begin to cover their assignments since it is a sprint action, but the quarterback hands the ball to the deep tailback. What makes this play so effective is the delayed execution with the good sprint-out quarterback action. The linebackers are striving for depth, and with the sprint look, the tailback receives the ball running full speed as he secures the hand-off (Diagram 4-13).

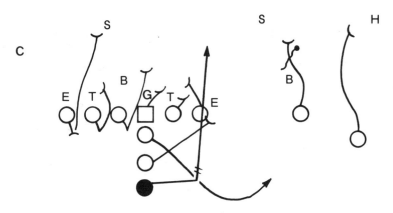

Diagram 4-13
The Sprint-Out Draw

ATTACK WITH THE READING DRAW

The same principle presented for reading blitzing linebackers during the passing game can be applied to the draw play as well. As indicated in Diagram 4-14, a flanker-split end set is shown versus the Pro-4 Defense. On the snap of the football, the quarterback drops back as if to pass and expects to give the ball to the offensive halfback. As long as the middle linebacker covers his same responsibility, the quarterback will commit the ball to his halfback. If, however, the linebacker stunts to rush the passer, which creates blocking difficulties for the offensive line, the quarterback will pull up and pass the ball to the tight end releasing inside. The tight end is keying the middle linebacker as well.

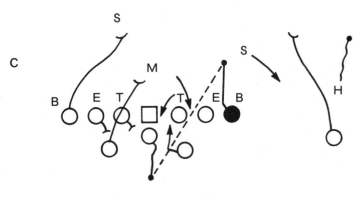

Diagram 4-14
The Reading Draw

ATTACK LINEBACKERS WITH THE SCREEN PASS

The screen pass is a beneficial component of the passing game versus defensive linebackers. It is especially advantageous if the linebackers are blitzing the quarterback. When stunting occurs, the linebackers and linemen, in effect, remove themselves from the play automatically. The quarterback must be a good actor. Once he is in the position to pass he should begin to retreat, as if scrambling away from the rush. If the linebackers are not stunting, however, the screen can be just as effective. As the linebackers are flowing back to their respective responsibilities, offensive linemen are forming in an area with a back or end setting behind them. Once the linebackers do recognize the screen, there are enough blockers to protect the receiver.

Screens can be executed from the dropback and sprint-roll-out action. Screens can evolve over the middle or to either side of the formation. Even wide outside to the flanker and split end areas are utilized. The coach should recognize the best areas to throw a screen pass. Knowing them and where to execute a screen becomes significant if a team is going to be successful. Is the rush coming from the middle or near the corners? Are linebackers gaining depth to one side of the field or the other?

Another effective screen is the play action screen pass. This is distinctly effective because it can maintain linebackers on the line of scrimmage for a relatively long period of time, with the pass being thrown in another area. A profitable play action screen is throwing quickly outside, with the play action fake inside occupying the linebackers. A dropback screen outside is indicated versus a stunting defense in Diagram 4-15, while Diagram 4-16 illustrates a

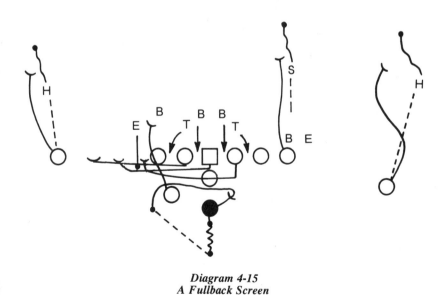

Diagram 4-15
A Fullback Screen

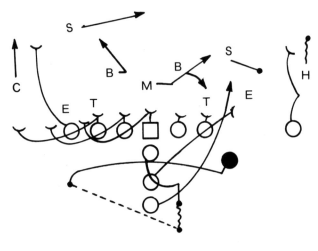

Diagram 4-16
A Play Action Screen

play action screen pass to a slot back. Regardless of the screen called, proper timing from the backs and linemen is necessary. A considerable amount of drilling is important in order for the screen to achieve success.

ATTACKING THE FLAT AREAS

The flat zones of a defense can be protected by either linebackers, defensive ends or secondary personnel rotated forward into a Monster scheme. Similar coverages can be utilized to a flanker-tight end formation or a split end set. There are basically three different alignment coverages with variations in the flat zone. Attacking this area will be determined by the three alignments.

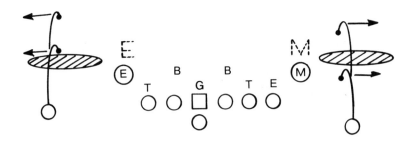

Diagram 4-17

The Closed Alignment

Diagram 4-17 illustrates the closed coverage toward the flanker and split end formation. Since the defensive alignment is tight on or near the line, the offense should attack the outside sector of the flat. The hitch, outside hook, quick-out, and square-out routes can be executed. For better success, other receivers can also release to occupy or hold the defender responsible for the flat.

The Walkaway Alignment

The walkaway position is shown in Diagram 4-18 with the areas of attack. In this situation the quick-out and square-out routes can be employed, although the quick hitch is not recommended. If the hook or curl route is considered, the wide receiver should adjust his route according to the movement and reactions of the walkaway defender (Diagram 4-19). If another receiver is released toward the flat to retain the walkaway defender's width, the better results occur with the routes mentioned. Diagram 4-20 illustrates an offensive back accelerating upfield as the split end executes an out route. Other route and pattern combinations can be used to force the offense into desired positions.

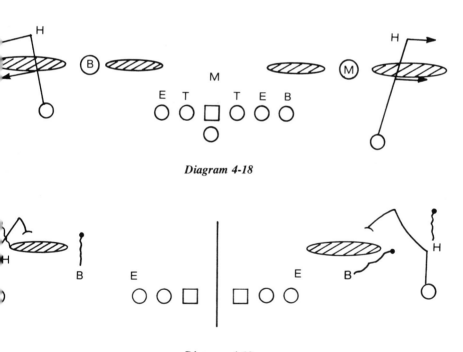

Diagram 4-18

Diagram 4-19

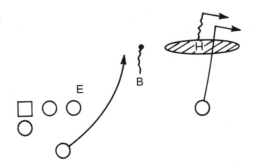

Diagram 4-20

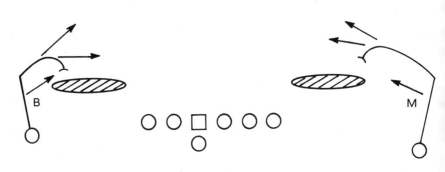

Diagram 4-21

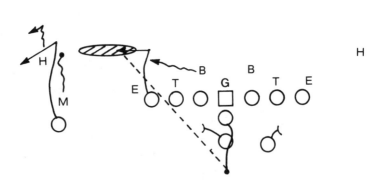

Diagram 4-22

The Wide Alignment

In some instances, the defense will widen as the receiver spreads, and will cover him directly on the line of scrimmage. Various positions can be attained (inside shoulder, outside shoulder, or head up, etc.). Regardless of the alignment, however, the defensive weakness areas occur inside. The best patterns include the curl, square-in, short post and slant (Diagram 4-21).

The offense can also attack with the inside receivers in the hook-curl areas. The outside defender can be occupied with the wide-out. Diagram 4-22 illustrates one of many patterns that are used versus this coverage. The flanker releases outside and executes an out route hoping to occupy the Monster defender. The tight end releases outside also, gains depth upfield, and immediately turns out to the vacated area indicated.

5

Coaching High-Scoring

Pass Routes

To produce a high-scoring passing attack, an offense must have at its disposal a multiplicity of pass routes and patterns. With competent and efficient pass defenses, it is essential for a sophisticated pass offense to be developed and established. The offense must defeat zones, man-to-man, various combinations of both, half coverages, etc. In order to acquire any degree of success, every design of attack must be at the finger tips of the coach. He should have the flair and capability to call various formations and release any number of receivers to a side, including one, two, three and possibly even four. This would be to both the strong and weak side of the set. Different pass actions should be prepared. A high scoring pass offense would include variations of the dropback pass, sprint-out and roll-out action. On top of this, play action passes must be installed to enhance the running game.

Pass routes of various widths and depths must be readily available. Field areas to attack are easily seen in Diagram 5-1. The field is separated into four main depth categories, as illustrated. Short, medium and long pass areas are across the line of scrimmage, while the swing and shuffle portions of the field are located on the offensive side. Pass routes to attack these areas, therefore, must be prepared well in advance. Routes to attack short, medium, or long are categorized to assist in developing successful patterns. Some patterns can be entirely short, and others entirely long. Other routes will be geared to attack one side of the field only. For example, three receivers could be released to one side of the field. One could be sent short, one medium and the other long.

LONG OUTSIDE 1/3	LONG MIDDLE 1/3	LONG OUTSIDE 1/3
MEDIUM OUTSIDE 1/3	MEDIUM MIDDLE 1/3	MEDIUM MIDDLE 1/3
SHORT OUTSIDE 1/3	SHORT MIDDLE 1/3	SHORT OUTSIDE 1/3
———O O O ☐ O O O———	O	
SWING	SHUFFLE	SWING

Diagram 5-1

As previously stated, a variety of pass routes must always be available. When the coach recognizes where each pass route can successfully attack specific areas, he will be better prepared to formulate game plans and make game adjustments on the sidelines. Game modifications and innovations are necessary due to different defensive linebacker and secondary alignments, reactions, and coverages.

THE PASS TREE

Regardless of the width and depth alignment on the field, pass cuts will be similar, although a few may vary slightly. This is due, of course, to the receiver's relationship to the formation, sideline and goal line. The split end and flanker routes are different than those of the tight end or slot back. The offensive halfback's routes will be altered because he is releasing from the backfield. Routes also vary due to the different defensive looks that occur opposite the receiver's alignment.

The pass tree from the various positions is illustrated in Diagram 5-2. The wide receiver's routes include the quick-out, hitch, slant, hook, curl, hook and out, hook and in, square-out, comeback, up, flag, post, and square-in. The inside receiver's routes comprise the hook, square-out, square-in, flag, streak, post, drag, flat and cross. The offensive halfback's routes include the flare, swing, flat, and circle.

Every pass route is separated into the short, medium, and long category for the purpose of attacking areas properly. Also, this categorization helps to familiarize the coach with the purposes the route is designed to achieve.

1.   Short routes include: the hitch, quick-out, slant, flare, swing, flat, circle, and drag.

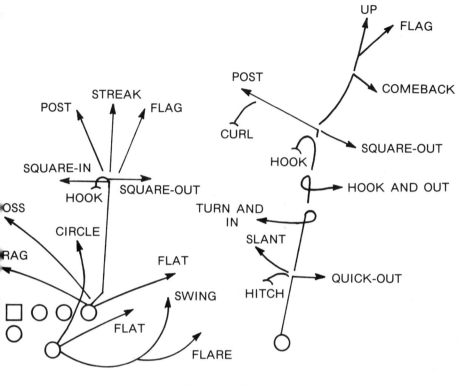

Diagram 5-2

2. Medium routes include: the hook, turn and in, hook and out, square-in, square-out, and cross.

3. Long routes comprise: the comeback, flag, up, streak, post, hook and go, etc.

The depths of these routes will be determined, for the most part, on the capability of the quarterback to throw the ball accurately. The receiver's ability to obtain freedom and his speed to get to the desired location are essential. The offensive linemen's efficiency to halt the pass rushers' momentum and keep them away from the quarterback will also determine the depths of the routes called. In many cases, the down and distance situations and the pass coverages employed will determine the depth. All of these points must be contemplated before any accurate pass route's depth can be ascertained.

THE IMPORTANCE OF WIDTH

A significant aspect of the passing game that can be drilled upon daily is the gaining of width from the formation as the release is made from the line. The greater width a receiver can attain, the greater the defense will have to spread out, and wider vacated areas will result within a zone. Considerable width can be attained by alignment alone. This is due to the formation, but it can be achieved once the play has started also. The receivers stretch apart, causing more difficulty for the defenders to assist each other on a pass. Receivers do not bunch together. Therefore, it becomes more difficult for the underneath and deep secondary to cover a pattern.

ATTAINING POSITION ON A DEFENDER

Once the receiver's release has been initiated, some coaches desire a face or head up relationship to the defender. The reason is that the receiver can drive inside or outside without having a defender gain a position either way. Attaining this position on a defender is especially good versus man-to-man coverages. The receiver can maneuver in either direction and with a slight head or shoulder fake, may increase his chances of getting open.

Another method to achieve an advantage on a defender is to force him in one direction but then go the other way. For example, if the receiver desires a square-out route he can release inside, causing the defender to turn his shoulder in that direction so he can run with and cover the receiver. However, the receiver then cuts outside and the defender must turn to cover him. This method is not always utilized a great deal because width is not attained. Offenses that face a great deal of man-to-man do find it worthwhile though. More alignment width may be essential so that the relationship with other receivers stays intact.

Releasing from the Line

Proper releasing techniques from the line of scrimmage are very important to a pattern's success. Definite depth and width yardage are necessary for openings to occur. If the receiver's release is slowed down, it may disrupt the success of the pattern. The receiver must release as rapidly and vehemently as he can off the line. Quickness on the count is essential. Once the initial takeoff has been achieved, quickness and speed, to gain the required yardage before any change of pace or cut is made, are imperative. If the pass receiver is bumped or shoved from his route, he must veer back as quickly as possible. If he is pushed and remains on his altered course, the relationship of his route to the other patterns may jeopordize the play. He must fight to stay on his avenue of travel. This should be drilled every day in order for good pass patterns to succeed. Various releases can be executed, including head, head and shoulder, stepping in one direction and going in another, spinning, etc.

PASS ROUTES

Various pass routes will be explained and illustrated in detail. Fundamentals, techniques, and coaching points for each route will also be included. Since most routes release outside this will not be mentioned again. The various pass routes will be classified into three main categories, which include the following:

1. The Quick Passes
2. The Outside Routes
3. The Inside Routes

The Quick Pass Routes

The Quick-Out (5 Yards)

The quick-out route is effective versus defensive halfbacks aligned deep off the line, or when the flat is covered inside. The quick-out is a four or five step route executed as rapidly as possible. The last step is completed with the inside foot so that it can plant, stop any momentum forward, and pivot outside. The receiver will come back toward the line of scrimmage slightly. The shoulders should be turned toward and parallel to the neutral zone. This enables the receiver to catch any pass low or behind him.

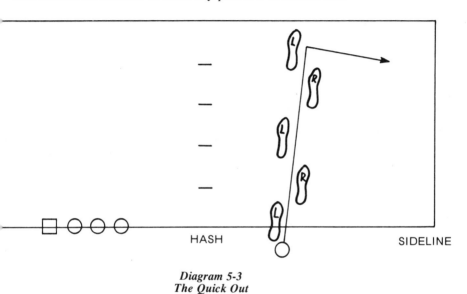

Diagram 5-3
The Quick Out

The Hitch (5 Yards)

The hitch is the most quickly executed pass route. The purpose of the hitch is to strike the receiver fast, when there is no defender covering nearby.

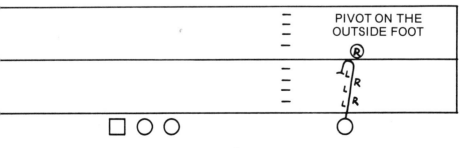

Diagram 5-4
The Hitch

No underneath coverage should be directly on him or located in a walkaway alignment. The wide-out will release downfield right away. A quick burst of speed should get him to the five yard position in a matter of a split second. He must plant with his outside foot (the sixth step if releasing with the inside foot), lower his center of gravity and make a complete rotated pivot on that foot. He should sight himself toward the quarterback, and angle his shoulder square to him. Remaining in a good ready position, he should flex his knees and have his hands prepared to catch the ball. With his back turned to the defensive halfback, he must be cautioned for a blow or tackle from behind. Positioning low and ready will enable him to catch the ball and hold onto it.

The Quick Slant (5 Yards)

The purpose of the quick slant is to drill the ball to the wide receiver rapidly, especially when there are no defenders covering the inside portion of the flat. The receiver will release on the same angle as the hitch. If his first step was initiated with the inside foot, then the fourth step will be planted with the outside foot. He automatically will push from this foot and look directly inside to the quarterback. The angle of the slant will be approximately 45 degrees. If the ball is not thrown on the fifth or sixth step, the receiver should immediately drive upfield, still glancing toward the quarterback. By maneuvering upfield, he has less of a risk of bumping into inside linebacker coverage, causing a possible interception. As with the other quick passes faking is not involved. Essentially, the quickness of the route is what exploits the defenders.

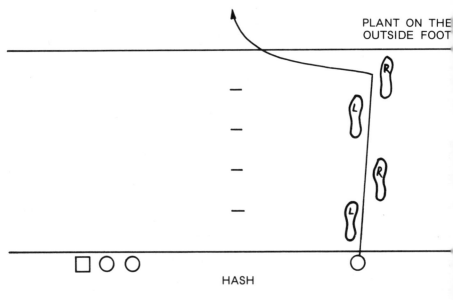

Diagram 5-5
The Quick Slant

The Outside Routes

The Square-Out (10 to 13 Yards)

The square-out route is a relatively safe pass, whether it is used versus man-to-man or zone. As long as defensive linebackers do not fall underneath it, the square-out has a good chance for success. Quarterback strength and accuracy is the significant factor. It is a long pass that must be thrown with good speed and acceleration, so the defensive halfback does not have time to react to the ball.

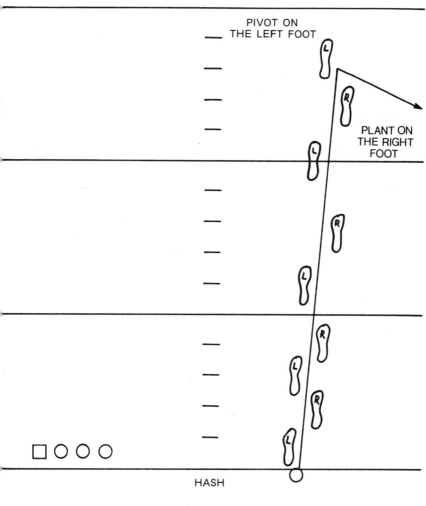

Diagram 5-6
The Square-Out

The receiver initiates an outside release, aiming for a point of approximately 10 to 13 yards. A sharp and quick cut to the sideline must be carried out. As the receiver approaches the required depth to angle out, he should plant his outside foot solidly and shift his center of gravity rearward. Since he is running at full speed, he should jerk his shoulders and head backwards, so as he digs in, the hips rotate forward. Flinging his arm up in the air in order to achieve this braking action is a coaching point. The next step is taken with the inside foot. This is the pivot, but also serves to help halt the receiver even more, if not done so after the outside foot was initially planted. If he is under control at this time, the receiver could utilize some faking action (head or head and shoulder fake) inside, hoping to get a reaction from the defensive halfback. As the inside step is planted, the receiver will pivot to the sideline and drive back toward the line of scrimmage at a sharp angle. His shoulders should become square or parallel to the chalk line, so if the ball is badly thrown, he still has the opportunity to catch it.

Photograph 5-1
The Square-Out Route

Notice the outside foot plants to avoid any momentum forward. The inside foot is used to halt further movement and to pivot outside. The head snaps around and the eyes scan the quarterback. The shoulders are parallel to the line of scrimmage so the receiver has the ability to catch any badly thrown ball.

There are a few coaches who neither teach the plant step with the outside foot, nor the second step which was used as a pivot, nor the head and shoulder fake—but do assist in halting any momentum forward. These coaches teach and drill to stop and plant with the inside foot only. More speed is accomplished with this method, but a sharp angle outside does become difficult. Photograph 5-1 illustrates the release, approach, cut, and follow-through of the square-out route.

When the receiver approaches the sideline and the ball has not been thrown, he should attempt to "hang" in this position, unless the defender has covered him well. If this is the case, he should begin sliding toward the middle of the field and attempt to locate any vacated areas.

The Comeback (16 to 19 Yards)

The comeback route is developed from the quick-out and up route. It is utilized to force the defensive halfback as deep as possible (as if it was the up route), but then it is instantly broken sharply toward the sideline. It must be well timed by the quarterback and receiver. The passer must accelerate the ball vigorously beyond the underneath coverage, but in front of the defensive halfback.

The receiver releases from the line and performs a rounded quick-out route with little faking involved. Once the break upfield is made, the receiver should sprint at full speed and drive to a distance between 16 and 19 yards. He

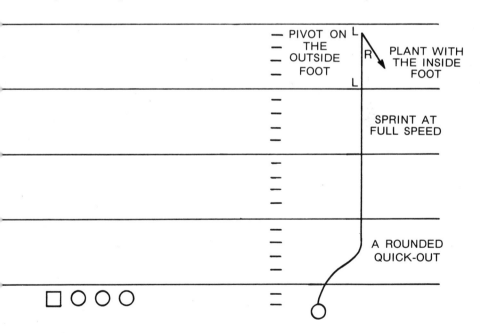

The Comeback Route

wants the defensive halfback to believe he is trying to beat him deep. Once he has the defender running at full speed, he will immediately bend the pattern toward the sideline. This is similar to the square-out, except there are no fakes involved. The faking occurred as he was sprinting with the up route. Throwing the weight forward and making a sharp turn is of utmost importance. The receiver drives back toward the line of scrimmage and ''hangs'' for the ball. Keeping the shoulders parallel, and staying in a good ready position, are both important coaching points as he scans inside to the quarterback.

The Up Route

The up route's purpose is to whip the defensive halfback deep. This may be exploited to get a quick touchdown, or to drive the defender deep so some other receiver can emerge underneath for the pass.

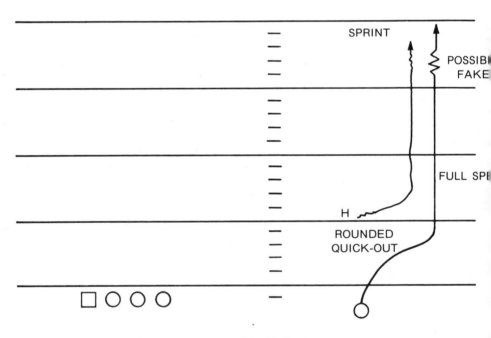

The Up Route

The up route is executed in a fashion similar to that of the comeback route. A looped quick-out is initiated after the release. Once the receiver turns upfield, it is a full sprint with hopes of beating the defender to the goal line. If the comeback pattern is executed a few times, a fake of the comeback can be undertaken around the 19 yard mark. This may slow the defensive halfback just enough in order for the receiver to outrace him. As the wide-out is sprinting, he should glance over his inside shoulder for the pass.

The Flag Route (Deep)

The release technique of the flag route is similar to the square-out. The cut is initiated around the 10 or 12 yard mark. The receiver aims for the corner of the field or flag which is a 45 degree angle from his drive upfield. There are two methods from which the flag route is taught. The first manner is for the receiver to pivot on his outside foot and initiate a course toward the post. On the third step, the receiver pivots on his inside foot and aims for the flag. The purpose of this zigzag maneuver is to force the defensive halfback to run inside or toward the post. The receiver will then angle toward the flag, hoping to gain a step or two on the defender. A second teaching method is to approach the cutting area, and without faking inside, pivot off the inside foot directly toward the flag. A head or shoulder fake could be adopted. The difference between the two techniques is that the three step fake demands a slightly longer period of time to accomplish. Certain patterns may be advantageous for this, while others will not. The receiver will continue toward the flag and look for the ball over his outside shoulder. Photograph 5-2 indicates the flag route.

Photograph 5-2
The Flag Route

After the release and sprint for approximately 10-12 yards, the receiver pushes off with his outside foot to fake a post route. Three steps are executed before pivoting with the inside foot, aiming him on a flag course.

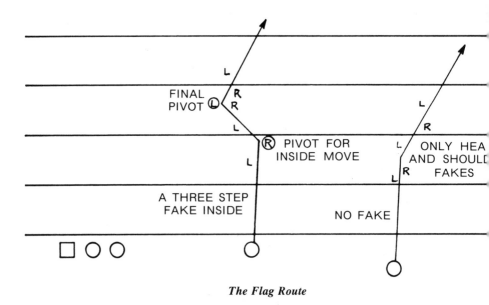

The Flag Route

The Inside Routes

The Curl (15-18)

The curl is a widely utilized pass route because of its ability to drift in open areas underneath linebacker coverage, its simplicity of execution, and the quarterback's relationship to it. It usually applies to the wide-out receivers only.

The receiver releases from the line of scrimmage and sprints at maximum speed for approximately 10 to 12 yards. As he approaches this juncture he will decelerate slightly, push off his outside foot, and break toward the post. The only fake involved may be a head motion or shoulder action outside. Once this action has taken place, he will begin to sprint toward the post. However, on his fourth step, or outside foot, the receiver must plant it solidly, launch his weight backwards as described previously, and drive toward the quarterback for two or three steps. This last maneuver or follow-through will open a cushion between the defensive halfback and himself.

As the third step is instituted the wide-out should break down into a good football ready position, keeping the shoulders square to the line of scrimmage, with a wide base, knees flexed, head up and hands in position to catch the ball. This ready position offers an opportunity to catch any ball thrown badly, whether it is low, high or to either side of him. His final position may have to be adjusted. This is due to the defensive underneath coverage and vacated areas presented. Sliding left or right and flowing away from linebackers must be attained. For example, if the defensive linebacker is positioned by the

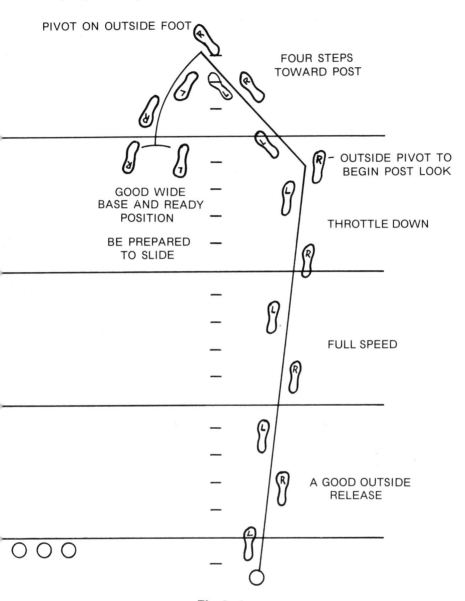

PIVOT ON OUTSIDE FOOT

FOUR STEPS
TOWARD POST

— OUTSIDE PIVOT TO
BEGIN POST LOOK

GOOD WIDE
BASE AND READY
POSITION

THROTTLE DOWN

BE PREPARED
TO SLIDE

FULL SPEED

A GOOD OUTSIDE
RELEASE

The Curl

wide-out's right shoulder, the curl receiver should slide left. The quarterback
must lead him in this direction. When this is put into practice, it is difficult for
the defender to hinder or intercept the football. Photograph 5-3 illustrates the
action of the curl route.

Photograph 5-3
The Curl Route

*The receiver sprints 10-12 yards before
pivoting toward a post course. After four
steps are executed, the receiver plants and
pivots back toward the quarterback. As
shown, he sets in a good football position
in order to catch the ball. He should scan
the underneath coverage in preparation to
shuffle away from it.*

The Post

The post route's intent is to attack the deep middle areas of the field. It is
an excellent route especially when the zone defenders are spread and must
either rotate or invert farther (because of formation width) in order to cover
the area. It is also good versus man-to-man defenses if the receiver has a step
and/or an angle between the quarterback and the defensive halfback.

As mentioned with the flag route, there are two techniques that can be
taught with the post pattern. The more complicated and time consuming
method is for the receiver to add some finesse to the route. The receiver
releases from the line and sprints on a course just like the flag or square-out.
After approximately 10 to 12 yards he decelerates slightly, so he can push
with his inside foot in order to drive outside. Once the break has occurred, the
receiver initiates three steps in the direction of the flag. However, on the third
step he pivots and turns upfield for the post on nearly a 60 degree angle toward
the goal line. Once the final cut has taken place, the receiver sprints at utmost
speed and adjusts his route only when necessary. This is according to the

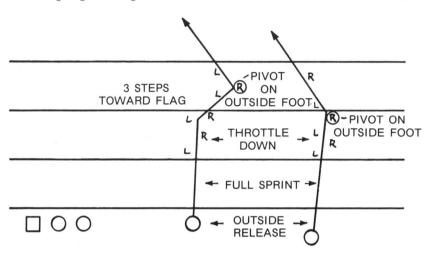

The Post Route

defensive coverage used. He should glance over his inside shoulder for the pass.

The second teaching method for the post pattern is to sprint at full speed until the breaking position is reached. He throttles down slightly at this point. A head or head and shoulder fake can be executed also. The receiver pivots with his outside foot and continues on the post course.

The Square-In (10 to 13 Yards)

The square-in is a good inside route for over the middle and curl areas. It is also advantageous versus man-to-man coverages because the receiver is continually moving away from the defender.

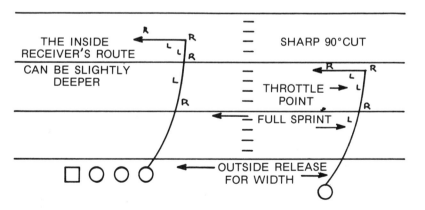

The Square-In

The receiver releases as he did with the square-out. A maximum sprint is needed along with a deceleration near the cutting juncture. Weight should be hurled backward in order for the pivot to be sharp, quick, and at 90 degrees. The pivot step is made by the outside foot, and will aim the receiver toward the middle of the field. He should continue on this plain and may have to adjust his speed according to the defensive coverage used. The shoulder should turn toward the quarterback or parallel to the line so he has the opportunity to grab any badly thrown ball. The inside receiver's depth can be slightly deeper because of his distance and relationship with the quarterback.

The Hook (10 to 13 Yards)

The hook pattern is utilized more versus zone than man-to-man defenses. If man-to-man is used, the receiver has the opportunity to slide in either direction to stay distant from the defensive halfback.

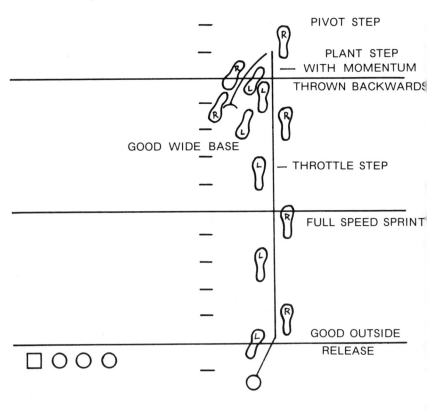

The Hook Route

The receiver will sprint approximately 10 to 13 yards downfield. Again, there are two methods for teaching the hook pattern. For a precise and well executed route, it is best for the hook receiver to begin his deceleration before the foot is planted. The receiver should solidly halt with the *inside* foot. He should lower his body and center of gravity, fling the head, shoulders, and inside arm backwards, and bring the hips forward. The next step (the pivot) is with the outside foot. It is utilized to check extra momentum and/or to initiate any body fake. The pivot step turns the receiver completely around to face the quarterback. Three added steps toward the passer are essential. The receiver should be in a good ready position for any pass thrown and/or have the ability to slide left and right away from the underneath coverage.

The other hook technique is for the receiver to sprint and throttle as mentioned, except only one step is utilized to both halt the receiver's momentum forward and pivot the body around toward the quarterback. This is taken by the outside foot. The depth of the receivers will be dependent upon the width of alignment. The depth of the outside wide receivers will usually be shorter than the inside receivers. Photograph 5-4 indicates the hook route.

Photograph 5-4
The Hook Route

As can be seen, the receiver plants with the inside foot in order to halt momentum forward. The outside foot is then used to pivot and push back toward the quarterback.

The Turn and In (10 to 13 Yards)

The turn and in is a variation of the square-in and hook routes. More faking and deception is utilized, and it is good against both the zone and man-to-man coverages.

The receiver sprints at maximum speed downfield approximately 10 to 13 yards. He reduces his speed slightly before the cut is initiated. The plant

PIVOT ON INSIDE FOOT

THROTTLE DOWN

GOOD OUTSIDE
RELEASE

The Turn and In

Photograph 5-5
The Turn and In Route

The receiver plants and drives with the inside foot to the sideline. Two steps are taken before he pushes back in the opposite direction, reading underneath coverage.

and pivot is made with the inside foot. The receiver casts his weight backwards to eliminate his momentum. He will pivot *outside* and bring the outside foot around facing the passer, as if a wide base is to be established. This entire action should be instituted in one flowing motion. He should then push inside to start himself on an inside course. From a defensive standpoint, the first action looks similar to an outside hook. However, the receiver continues inside and continually scans for the ball. Photograph 5-5 illustrates the action and execution of the turn and in route.

Other Routes

There are numerous other pass routes an offense can utilize. However, there isn't a great deal of cutting or a specific technique involved. What is important, however, is the position on the field the receiver maintains in relation to the defensive coverage and the other offensive receivers. Some of these routes include the flat, swing, flare, circle, drag and cross. Timing and proper positioning are important and must be drilled and practiced every day.

Decoys

Many pass patterns are developed with primary and secondary receivers. If a player is not designated to be a prime receiver, he should still continue his route properly. Executing it halfheartedly can easily be indicated to the pass defense. The quarterback may want to throw to the secondary receiver. It is essential, therefore, that each receiver execute his responsibility as if he were the prime prospect for the entire pattern.

PASS RECEIVING COACHING POINTS

The following list includes good coaching points for every receiver.

1. Align in a good stance to achieve a good start at the snap. Use the same stance whether it is for a run or a pass.

2. Explode out from the position as quickly and fast as possible.

3. Do not be held in by a defender. Read the alignment of the defender before the snap of the football so it becomes easier to release.

4. If bumped off course, get back on it. Never remain on the course shoved into. Relationships with the other receivers and defensive coverage are essential to the success of the patterns. Force back to the proper lanes.

5. All pattern angles should be initiated sharply except when fakes must be accomplished. It becomes easier for the defenders to cover the route if done haphazardly.

6. Use your body weight and control. Learn how to halt and decelerate momentum in different directions.

7. Once the break has been established, remain on good stride and glance toward the passer.

8. Watch the ball all the way into the hands. Give with the ball slightly to ensure a good catch.

9. Always use two hands for the catch. Once the ball is caught, put the ball away. Do not carry it away from the body.

10. You may be tackled immediately once the ball is caught. However, if not, be prepared to use good ball carrying techniques as you begin to drive upfield.

SYSTEMS OF CALLING PATTERNS

There are various and numerous methods to call pass routes and patterns. Some are more difficult than others. The coach should find the best system for his program and fit it into his offense. For a high-scoring pass offense, simplicity, at times, is not the key. A system must often be employed with many routes, patterns, formations, and quarterback actions so it can attack a defense strategically with preciseness and swiftness.

Numbered Routes

A few coaches prefer to number their offensive pass routes, and have the opportunity to call a thousand-and-one patterns. Game adjustments can easily be utilized, maintained and innovated with this system, since a number is all that must be called. The action of the quarterback is also included with the numbering system.

Name Routes

A few offenses apply the same sort of system except names are given with the routes. Each receiver must know and understand what route he is to execute. The offense uses a "key" for this. For example, the split end is known as "X," the tight end is "Y," and the flanker is called "Z." A pattern stated in the huddle, therefore, would be "X-Post, Y-Hook, Z-Curl."

Letter Routes

As was mentioned with the numbering or name system, letters can be used for routes. The quarterback calls the letters that are designated routes and a system is developed.

Series

An often adopted system is to furnish each action of the quarterback a series number, and then add a number for a particular pattern. For example, the 50 series is the sprint-out, while the 60 series is the quick dropback and the 70 series is the regular dropback. If the deeper dropback were desired, then the numbers 70 through 74 are patterns to the formation side, while 75 through 79 are routes to the weak side. Therefore, there are five patterns to either flank and rote memory is used to remember each one. A "71" route may have the flanker square-out, tight end hook and halfback swing. The "72," however, would be completely different. If a variation of the entire pattern is desired, it can be easily called. An example would be the "71" pattern. The quarterback calls "71-Flanker Up." The flanker executes an up route, but the tight end and halfback remain the same.

6

Reading and Controlling

Passing Defenses

Reading and keying defensive pass coverages is a profitable method in attaining success with a high-scoring passing offense. The extent to which reading is established within the offensive system will be determined by the quarterbacks' and receivers' capability and proficiency to grasp the entire understanding of it. Considerable practice and mental time is essential to install a reading offensive system. Reading and keying of defensive schemes can be simplified or complex. The entire reading aspects of defensive pass coverages will be explained in complete detail. A coach can adopt a few or many of the ideas presented. If practice time is not a factor with the details of a reading system, then substantially more can be introduced to the offensive pass system. It is emphasized, however, that some form of reading and/or keying of the pass defense be utilized by an offense. A great degree of error is eliminated because the offensive pattern called can adjust or even change due to the pass defense shown. Interceptions and incompletions can be reduced to a minimum.

Reading can be realized with any pass offensive game. It can be utilized by the sprint and roll-out attack, quick passing games, dropback and all play action passes. It should be understood that the entire defensive secondary play does not have to be scanned in order to pass the football. Only one defender has to be read or keyed in order to throw. Therefore, only one portion of the field must be focused on by the quarterback. Of course, additional reads can be achieved as the offense gains experience, but they will be added only as the offense matures.

POSITION READING

There are fundamentally three categorical alignments within the offense which have the capability to read pass defenses. They comprise the quarterback, quick receivers located on the line of scrimmage, and the offensive backs positioned in the backfield.

The Quarterback

The quarterback is the most important position in the reading game. If a limited degree of reading and keying is installed by a coach, the quarterback should be the first player to utilize it. If the offensive patterns do not adjust or change, at least the quarterback can understand defensive secondary principles and read whether the secondary is executing zone, man-to-man or a combination of these coverages. His knowledge assists him in knowing the weak and strong aspects of coverages, and the capability to locate secondary receivers if the primary route is covered. At times he may have to pass the ball out of bounds or beyond the defenders' heads so interceptions will not occur.

The introduction of additional reading forces the quarterback to more fully understand and realize how and when to employ various pass patterns. Also, his knowledge of pass defenses should not leave any degree of error. If mistakes are going to occur, they must not happen in the reading of pass defenses.

The Receivers

The quick receivers driving from the line of scrimmage can also be taught how to read secondary coverages. This can be accomplished either before and/or after the snap of the football. The degree of reading inaugurated will be determined by the mental capabilities and practice time available. A coach may desire reading only with one route or pattern. This can easily be achieved since the amount of teaching time involved is limited. If adjustments to patterns only are necessary, the quarterback does not have to understand it because the route is not going to change substantially. He should know where the receiver will complete his route. Adjustments are exclusively a matter of depth and width, and the quarterback has the ability to alter his pass slightly.

The Offensive Backs

While the styles of patterns executed by the offensive backs from the backfield are rather limited in scope, there can be reading of defensive pass coverages. The quarterback does not have to worry about the adjustments, but he should realize any change in the route.

A Combination of Reads

The choice reading possibility is to have the quarterback, backs, and ends scan secondary coverages at the same time. This is not as difficult as it may sound. It must, however, be taught correctly with painstaking patience. Adjustments may be carried out individually. Changing patterns on the move may also be desired. Once the quarterback, backs, and ends know exactly the pattern called and each player completely understands his assignment, if the pass defense mobilizes a particular coverage, there shouldn't be any problem with reading.

Some pass systems may have the quarterback and ends reading and keying, while other systems may desire the backs and ends. Whatever the combination, it should be totally knowledgeable to the entire offense.

CONCEPTS OF READING AND CONTROLLING DEFENSES

There are actually two methods to attack various defensive weaknesses: *before* the ball is snapped, and *after*. This is accomplished in order to direct the best pass pattern or route toward the weakest areas of the defense. Considerable pass completions will occur and less mistakes, interceptions, and incompletions will be realized. Better passing percentages result, and an offense will have more confidence in the entire passing game.

Reading Before the Snap of the Football

Reading the secondary coverage before the snap of the football can be fulfilled in many situations. For example, man-to-man coverages can be read in certain situations. If there are two wide-outs aligned toward one side of the field versus a three or four deep, man-to-man can readily be noticed. The quarterbacks and receivers should see this defensive scheme, and should have the adjustment or alteration of the routes ingrained in their minds for instant referral. Other examples of reads and keys can be achieved with four spoke rotation and invert, three deep zones, etc. These are implemented entirely before the snap. Stunting can also be determined at times. Some teams desire stunting during man-to-man situations. If the offense reads the man-to-man concept, they can be prepared for the stunt in advance. Changing the play on the line of scrimmage can be realized when this occurs. This is also true with other defenses and patterns called. When a quarterback expects man-to-man, but notices zone, he may desire an alteration of the pattern before the snap is initiated.

Some teams desire similar pass routes to both sides of the field at the same time. For an example, if the flat areas are uncovered, the offense can attack the area with various pass routes, including the square-out, quick-out, hook, curl, etc. The quarterback steps to the center, glances to both flanks for the less covered receiver, and then passes to the one that is clearly open. Maximum blocking should be exercised with the line and backs. If the flat areas are uncovered, more stunting and blitzing could occur. Diagram 6-1 illustrates similar routes to both sides of the formation. Since the split end is covered by a walk-away linebacker, the quarterback turns and throws to the flanker side.

Reading After the Snap of the Football

Once the defensive team begins to cover the vacated areas shown before the snap, such as the flat areas described, the offensive team must read and key after the snap of the football for the reactions of the defense. For example,

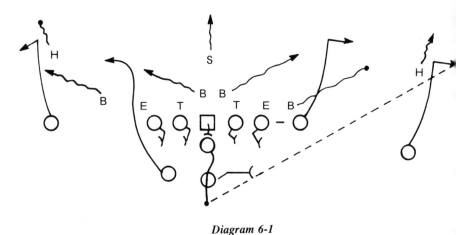

Diagram 6-1

if the defensive secondary rotates and the square-out route has been called, the route may desire alteration, as illustrated in Diagram 6-2. In this example, the reading offensive team believes it can control and attack the movements of the defense through pattern changes. If the defense adjusts one way, the offense will go the other. The offense, therefore, controls the various situations that occur, and has a better percentage and opportunity to complete a pattern than if reading were not adopted.

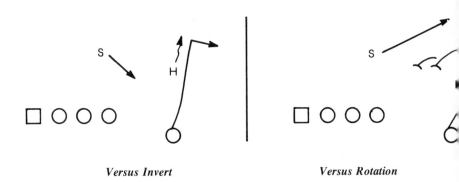

Versus Invert   *Versus Rotation*

Diagram 6-2

Development of Strategy

Strategy of a particular pattern can be developed by a coach. After formulating a pattern, he can take the coverages he observes during a season and create any adjustments or changes necessary with the receivers. This can be generated before and after the ball has been put into play. The coach must locate the best defender to key so that pattern adjustments or modifications can be made. They can be developed through the utilization of films, scouting and observations of defenses. Once these aspects are known, the coach can execute the passing routes and attack the defenders and coverages strategically. During game week, the quarterback, backs, receivers and interior linemen can prepare and drill versus the various movements and schemes of the defense.

Formation and Patterns

Formations can determine not only the type of patterns executed, but the coverages of defenses as well. The defenders can align in other positions, and secondary coverages can alter due to the width and depth of pass receivers and offensive backs. A pro formation with a split end and divided backfield is quite different than a wide slot to one side of the formation, a tight end toward the other, and an "I" backfield. Linebacker alignments and coverages will automatically alter. Defensive secondary play can easily change also. The various offensive routes and patterns must be employed from the formations necessary for their successful execution. An example is clearly shown. If a flanker-split end set is used versus a three deep defense the secondary will not rotate in most cases. However, once the split end is brought into a closed alignment, rotation can easily result. Some patterns, therefore, will not be as effective toward the rotation. In the same vein, if rotation is necessary for a particular pattern, the offense should not apply a two wide-out formation, but procure a tighter alignment.

Similar ideas can be devised with the offensive backfield. Linebacker coverage may not be able to cover a split backfield alignment as well as an "I" set. Offensive backs can release quicker, and the linebackers may not be in a good alignment to cover them. The defensive linebacker alignment would have to be altered which, therefore, could aid another route or portion of a pattern. Forcing a linebacker to adjust wider, for example, may benefit another receiver's route in the middle areas. In similar fashion, requiring a linebacker to remain inside may help a receiver on the outside portions of the field to find an opening. These slight, but important points, must be thoroughly analyzed well in advance. Various strategical ideas with regard to the variations and patterns of formations can greatly enhance success with the offensive passing game.

Strategy of Flow Actions

Backfield flow action can provide a distinct advantage for the offense. In many cases, linebackers and the defensive secondary key offensive backs positioned in the backfield. The offensive backs' movement in one direction or another will determine the coverage used. Flow action can alter zone and man-to-man looks, yielding beneficial information to the offense. The movement can be used to great advantage with any pass offense. Directional flow of the offensive backs is illustrated in Diagram 6-3. Linebacker coverage of these movements is also illustrated.

An example of backfield flow and its attacking value is indicated in

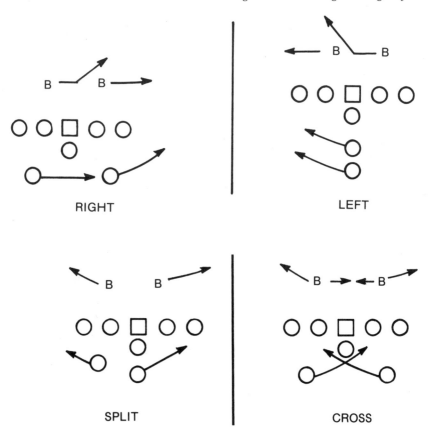

Diagram 6-3

Diagram 6-4. A regular backfield alignment flows left, with the middle linebacker from a Pro-4 Defense reacting in that direction. The pattern side, however, is located toward the flanker-tight end. Since a linebacker is eliminated from the pattern, the opportunity for success has increased. If the backfield course split or sweeped in the opposite direction, the middle linebacker may have reacted toward the designed pattern side.

Another example versus the defensive secondary is sprint-out action shown in Diagram 6-5. Both backs from the "I" formation·move toward the wide-slot, forcing rotation at that point. However, the quarterback sprints opposite the flow and defensive rotation, and has the opportunity to throw to either the split end or dragging slot back.

Various Methods of Reading After the Snap of the Football

There are four categories of reads for attacking defensive coverages.

1. Adjustment Reads

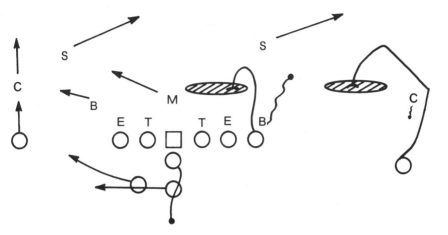

Diagram 6-4

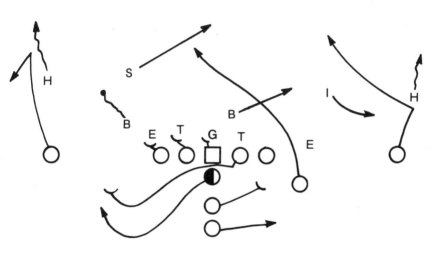

Diagram 6-5

2. Change Reads
3. The "Hot" Receiver Reads
4. A Combination

Adjustment Reads

Adjustment reads are executed by receivers only. A particular pattern is called by the quarterback. As the receivers align in the formation, they attempt to read the defensive coverage before the ball is snapped. Any hint of a particular coverage, because of the defensive alignment, may assist their route. However, if the coverage cannot be recognized, adjustments must be made as the receiver bursts from the line.

Adjustments do not involve changing one route to another. The same route is executed that was mentioned in the huddle. However, one or all routes can be slightly changed or modified in order to defeat the coverage observed. Adjustment reads are not difficult. The quarterback is cognizant of the route specified, and reads the adjustment and the receiver's open area. Adjustment reading can be created with any pattern, whether it is short, medium or long.

The curl route is a good example of reading underneath linebacker coverage. As the wide-out (Diagram 6-6) completes his breakoff back to the quarterback, he will "read" the first linebacker driving from the inside-out position toward his area. If the linebacker remains inside, the curl receiver can slide slightly outside. If the linebacker drives outside, the curl receiver can shuffle inside.

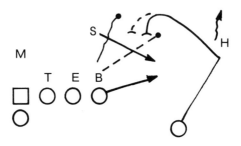

Diagram 6-6

Another example of the curl route is illustrated (Diagram 6-7) versus man-to-man coverage. As the receiver executes his curl and notices man-to-man coverage being utilized, he can begin accelerating inside. He attempts to sprint away from the defender so the quarterback is assured he has the opportunity to complete the pass.

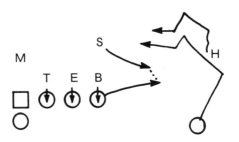

Diagram 6-7

The square-out can be adjusted easily also. The receiver runs his normal route versus most defenses—i.e., straight zone, invert, or man-to-man. However, if rotation is detected by the receiver where the defensive halfback is in direct line between the quarterback and himself, the receiver can correct his route by hooking out. He, therefore, has the advantage to slide in or out away from the revolved halfback or any other linebackers. In this case, the wide-out keys the defensive halfback as to whether he rotates forward or drops away from the line (Diagram 6-8).

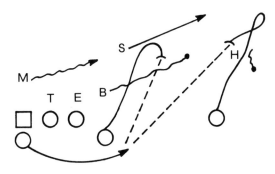

Diagram 6-8
A Square-Out Adjustment

Deep or long routes, such as the flag, up, and post, can be revised on the move also. A simple post route is indicated in Diagram 6-9. The wide receiver

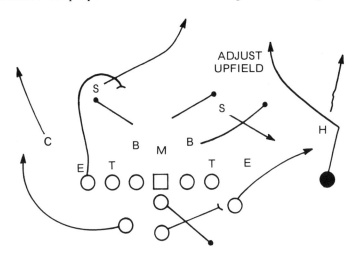

Diagram 6-9
A Post Route Adjustment

breaks toward the post and notices the safety has a good opportunity to cover him by rotating to the deep middle. The receiver will modify his route by aiming straight upfield, similar to a streak route. This slight shift helps the receiver to get open, eliminates interception possibilities, and provides a better chance for success.

Offensive backs releasing into the pattern also have the capability to adjust all their routes. Diagram 6-10 indicates one possibility. The halfback releases to the flat and keys the defender responsible for the area. In most cases, the offensive halfback reaches a depth of 3 to 5 yards. Since the flat is covered near the 5 yard stripe, the halfback does not gain depth, but sprints along the line of scrimmage. If the ball is thrown to him, he has the opportunity to catch it and turn upfield for yardage.

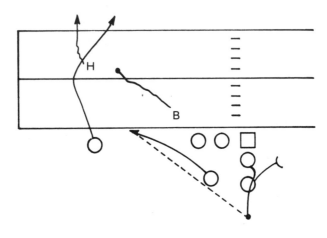

Diagram 6-10

Change Reads

Changing routes becomes much more difficult than just adjusting them. Both the receiver and quarterback must key particular defenders and execute quick judgments on the move. Since every route or pattern varies and attacks other areas, keying different defenders is possible. A vast amount of mental preparation must be accomplished so that proper reads of defensive coverages occur. Drills and practice time are significant in order to attain proper execution of the pattern.

There are many routes that can change due to the defensive coverages used. For example, a curl route can change to a post on the movements of the inside safety. The strong inside safety of a four spoke secondary can either rotate, invert or perform some type of man-to-man. An alternate receiver should be added to force a coverage desired in coordination with the curl. Diagram 6-11 illustrates the flanker turning a curl route to a post and the inside receiver, or tight end, springing toward the flat. The wide-out keys the

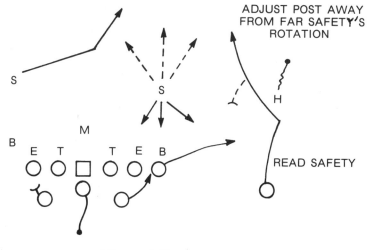

ADJUST POST AWAY
FROM FAR SAFETY'S
ROTATION

READ SAFETY

Diagram 6-11

inside safety as he releases. If the safety comes forward for any reason (to cover the tight end man-to-man or invert to the flat zone), the wide-out immediately changes his course to the post route. However, if the safety defender drops away or rotates to the deep outside 1/3 of the field, the flanker will complete his curl. Adjustment maneuvers after the route change will then have to be accomplished. If the post is executed, the flanker reacts according to the far (weak) safety's ability to cover the deep middle. If it is a curl, however, he then reads the underneath coverage (zone or man).

Another example of changing routes is illustrated in Diagram 6-12. The tight end releases to perform a square-out route and keys the strong side

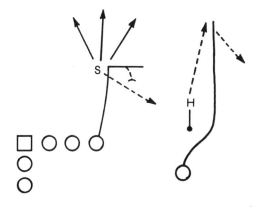

Diagram 6-12

safety. If the defender drops backward to play either man-to-man or rotation zone, the tight end will continue on the square-out course. If the defensive safety progresses forward as devised for invert coverage, the tight end halts his momentum outside and hooks out, keying the linebacker and safety zone courses. The wide-out flanker executes an up route and if he desires, can change his route also. His assignment keys the defensive halfback to his side. If the defensive halfback goes backward for any reason, the flanker sprints upfield and executes a comeback route. If the defensive halfback rotates forward, however, the flanker attempts to whip the revolving strong safety by sprinting to the corner. The quarterback keys the strong side safety only. If the safety drives toward the line of scrimmage, the flanker utilizes a comeback while the tight end executes a hook-out. His primary receiver on this pattern, however, is the tight end. Throwing deep to the flanker on his comeback route will only be an alternative if the tight end is not open.

There are various other routes and patterns that can also change. These patterns can be adopted to both the strong or weak side of a formation. Any quarterback and backfield action can be employed. As mentioned previously, linebacker coverage can be controlled by the backfield also. Such routes that can change are the quick-out to the up, flag to a square-out, post to a curl, hook to a square-in, etc.

The "Hot" Receiver Reads

There are many times when offenses desire to send four or five receivers on a pattern at a time. When this results, there are only five interior linemen positioned to block a six to eight man rush. If the rush occurs, a quarterback must have an outlet receiver. This is the "Hot" receiver principle and is usually only considered with the dropback pass. The sprint out action can use it, however. The "hot" receiver can be either an offensive halfback or end depending upon the pattern called.

The quarterback and "hot" receiver read linebackers once the ball is snapped. The proper linebacker read depends upon the defense. From the Pro-4 it is the middle linebacker, while from the 5-4 and 4-4 it is the first linebacker toward the side of the pattern. As the ball is centered, the quarterback retreats to the required depth and reads the movement of the linebacker. If he stunts forward or vacates away from the pattern side, the quarterback will deliver the ball to the "hot" receiver. However, if these linebacker reactions do not occur, the quarterback will *not* relinquish the ball. The "hot" receiver will key the same linebacker also. If he notices the linebacker moving forward or vacate away, he yells "hot-hot" to alert the quarterback he is open or free. The backs, ends and quarterback should drill and co-ordinate their play for the quick pass. The ball must be tossed quickly with force over the heads and arms of the defensive pass rushers. Diagram 6-13 illustrates the "Hot" receiver principle.

A Combination

Some teams utilize only the adjustment phase of reading. Other offenses employ a few or many route changes. Some coaches desire the "hot" receiver concept just mentioned. Yet some schools attempt to execute with all three

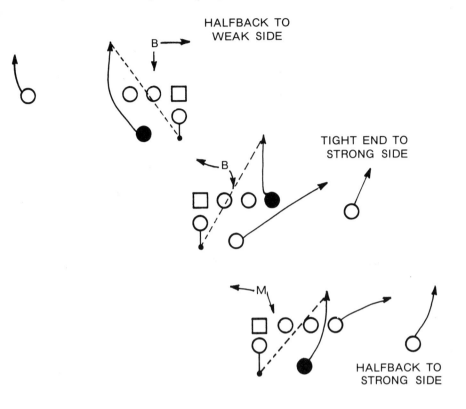

HALFBACK TO
WEAK SIDE

TIGHT END TO
STRONG SIDE

HALFBACK TO
STRONG SIDE

Diagram 6-13

methods. The quarterback, receivers, and offensive backs use this sophisticated attack by reading all the defensive reactions that occur in a game. For
example, the quarterback steps up to the ball and reads the defense before the
cadence is called. Linebackers and secondary alignments may give him a hint
of the coverage, or he may spot an immediate opening that he may prefer. He
also has the opportunity to change plays on the line of scrimmage. As the ball
is snapped, the quarterback drops back and reads the "hot" receiver. If there
is an opportunity to pass the ball quickly, because of the defensive reaction,
the quarterback will do so. If, however, it is not necessary to pass to the
"hot" receiver, the quarterback will immediately scan to his next key. The
quarterback must gauge the reactions of his receivers according to the secondary coverage observed. After the receivers release, they can change and/or
adjust their patterns to the defensive scheme used. The offensive backs also do
the same. This combination of keying and reading becomes a very specialized
method of attacking defenses. Drilling and practice time must be available in
order to fulfill all the requirements of the attack.

7

The Strong-Side Dropback
Passing Game

The strong-side dropback passing offense is directed toward the strength of the offensive formation. The quarterback sets to a position of seven to nine yards. The basic pass offense includes two receivers releasing to the strong side and one to the back side (Diagram 7-1). Wide-out formations provide good route and adjustment needs. The

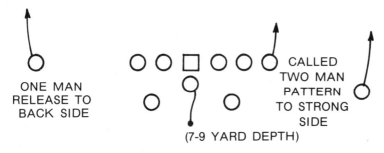

ONE MAN
RELEASE TO
BACK SIDE

CALLED
TWO MAN
PATTERN
TO STRONG
SIDE

(7-9 YARD DEPTH)

Diagram 7-1

back side can split an end, although this is not always necessary. The strong wide-out formation can utilize a flanker-tight end, wide slot, or twins look. Various splits and widths can be used to entice or alter the pass coverage. While the outside receiver usually has automatic width, it is good for the inside receiver to have split distance also. This can be a "nasty" split, as indicated in Diagram 7-2. The reason for this is obvious. The receiver has the opportunity to release inside or outside. If positioned tight, he can easily be delayed outside with very little area to release inside.

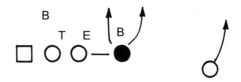

Diagram 7-2

TWO MAN PATTERNS

Two man patterns are specified to the offensive set's strength. Any number of patterns can be introduced. The back-side end executes the same route unless he is told otherwise (Curl). For example, if the offensive system uses the X, Y, and Z system for the receivers, the quarterback states in the huddle "Dropback, Y-Flag, Z-In." The "Dropback" sets the series and line blocking. The "Y" (tight end) runs a flag while the "Z" (Flanker) executes an in route. Since the back-side end's route is not altered in the huddle, he continues to carry out the curl. An ample amount of two man patterns can be utilized.

If the quarterback required a back-side alteration for the end, he could state in the huddle, "Dropback, Y-Hook, Z-Curl——X-Post." This is illustrated in Diagram 7-3. An innumerable number of pass patterns can ensue this way from the dropback series, with a minimum of words mentioned in the huddle.

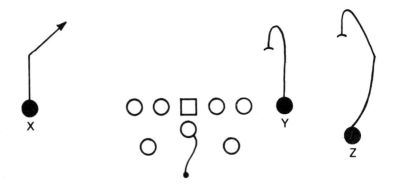

Diagram 7-3

FLARE CONTROL

One of the integral factors of the two man pattern dropback pass is the utilization of flare control by the offensive backs. Offensive backs key linebackers to either block or release. Maximum protection is given to the quarterback. If stunts are indicated, the backs are in position to restrain linebackers who rush. Although extra receivers may not be running in the pattern, a heavy rush is contained.

The offensive backs must be in proper alignment to key their respective linebackers and react quickly to their action. The backfield set is not significant. A deep tailback positioned in the "I" formation must move slightly quicker than if he was aligned in his normal backfield depth. However, this can be properly taught, drilled, and timed.

Flare Control Rules

The rules for flare control are rather easy for memorization.

1. Frontside Back—Check the first linebacker toward the side of the formation. If no rush occurs—FLARE.
2. Offside Back—Check the first linebacker from the center with an odd defense. If the defense is even, check the linebacker outside the tackle. If no rush occurs—FLARE.

Diagram 7-4 illustrates flare control rules versus the 5-4, Split-4, and Pro-4 Defenses. If a rush occurs with these linebackers, the backs must

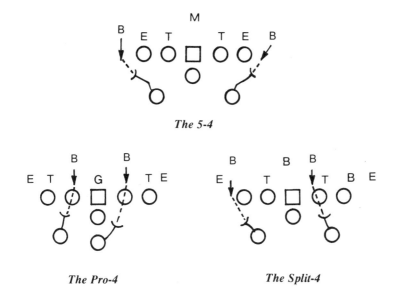

The 5-4

The Pro-4   *The Split-4*

Diagram 7-4

immediately step up as close to the line as possible and block the linebackers' rush away from the quarterback. The offensive back should remain low with a good wide base, knees flexed, arched back, bulled neck and head up. As contact is about to be made with the linebacker, he should jab step quickly and deliver a blow. His shoulders remain square to the linebacker. He should direct the linebacker's rush outside or away from the quarterback.

Flare Control Routes

If a rush does not occur, the offensive backs automatically release into the pattern. The read is quick, with the inside foot jabbing forward. If the linebacker does not blitz, he pivots and pushes to release. The flare control routes are determined upon the receiver aligned nearest to the back. If the receiver's route specified aims outside, the flare back releases inside. If the route called is geared inside, the flare control back sprints outside. The flare route utilized should control a linebacker or secondary defender. Certain defenders must position to cover the flare back. This automatically opens passing lanes for the basic pattern designated.

Only two flare control routes are necessary. One route is geared to go outside, while the other drifts inside. One fundamental outside flare route for backs is the swing (Diagram 7-5). If the nearest receiver route to him drives

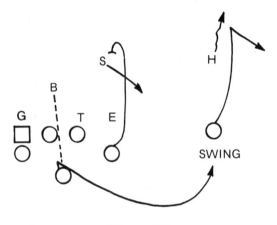

Diagram 7-5

inside, he automatically swings wide outside, expecting to control the defender responsible for the flat. If the receiver occupies the defender, other patterns should open. However, if the defender covers the primary route, the flare back should become free. Diagram 7-6 illustrates the circle route, with the nearest receiver sprinting to the outside areas. It is essential for him to read the inside linebacker's reactions as he clears upfield. If the linebacker remains with him, he should continue to lure the defender and, at the same time, have the opportunity to get open. However, if the linebacker sprints underneath

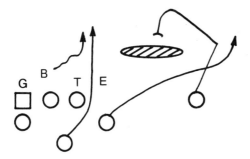

Flare with Circle–LB Stays with Him

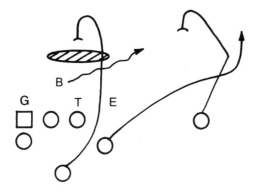

Flare with Circle–LB Overruns to Curl Area

Diagram 7-6

him to attain width, due to the design of the pattern routes, the back should halt and hook inside, offering the quarterback an opportunity to spot him free.

LINE BLOCKING

Dropback blocking rules are rather simplified. The following rules are for the tackles, guards, and center.

1. Tackles—Block the #2 Man on the Line of Scrimmage
2. Guards—Block the #1 Man on the Line of Scrimmage
3. Center—Block Over, Linebacker Offside, Check Frontside

1. Tackles

The tackle is responsible for the number 2 defensive rusher or lineman on the line of scrimmage. Before the ball is centered, the tackle counts from the center position out and spots the number 2 man.

2. Guards

The guards are assigned the number 1 man on the line of scrimmage. A quick glance at the defensive alignment before the snap will easily tell him who is the defender.

3. Center

The center blocks any defender aligned over him first. If there isn't anyone located there, he then scans to the first linebacker offside and blocks him if he rushes. If the defender does not blitz, the center will help protect frontside or the side of the pattern designated. Diagram 7-7 illustrates the blocking responsibilities versus four common defenses.

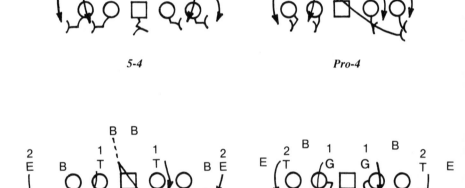

5-4   Pro-4

Split-4   Wide-6

Diagram 7-7

The style of block employed by the offensive linemen is passive at first. The linemen should have some concept of the defensive rush lanes. Since defenses are constantly changing, a lineman's assignment may force him wide on one play and inside on another. From a balanced offensive stance, the interior linemen will jab step inside to gain an inside-out approach or angle to the rusher. The line should try to drive the rushers outside as far as possible. This presents ample clearance to the quarterback to scan his receivers. As the jab step is initiated, the body remains low with the hips down, knees flexed, and head up.

The next step is taken with the outside foot. It is brought away from the line of scrimmage so that the body whirls outside toward the defenders' rush. As he terminates this step, the body should be low and in an advantageous football position. The base is wide for good balance. The knees are flexed, and the lineman is prepared to explode at the defender. The hips remain low and the back is arched in a profitable hitting position. The arms are completely flexed at the elbow, with the hands clenched as if set in a balanced boxer's stance. The elbows are in by the hips so that the defensive linemen cannot grab them and attempt to turn the blocker. The inside shoulder should be aimed toward the line of scrimmage, and the outside shoulder pointed away. This exaggerated turn and body posture definitely places the linemen in a sufficient angle position outside.

The blocker is now prepared to move. He should never cross his feet. He begins to shuffle backwards and to the outside. He should remain balanced and low. The feet are constantly in motion as if ''running in his shoes.'' This coaching point's purpose is not to instill choppy footwork. It does signify, however, to bring the heels off the ground in an up and down movement, as if running within the shoes. This continuous foot and leg movement results in a preparedness to take on the opponent. Photograph 7-1 indicates the techniques of this initial movement.

Photograph 7-1

In this sequence of photographs, the offensive lineman jab steps inside with his left foot. The body should remain low with the hips down, knees flexed and head up. Notice the body position, with the shuffling of the feet gaining an inside-out approach. The inside shoulder aims toward the line of scrimmage.

As the blocker is ready to "uncoil" into the rushing linemen, he must be in a good football position. Anytime the body is raised with the knees in a non-flexible position, the blocker does not have any exploding or uncoiling potential. As contact is about to be generated, the blocker springs forward and upward through the neck of the rusher. Timing is essential. The blocker cannot uncoil too quickly, or he will extend farther than necessary, and a good hit, therefore, cannot be established. In the same fashion, the blocker cannot wait until the last instant, when the defender is almost over him. If he attempts to attack up and through the rusher, he will only be shoved back. If, however, the blocker times his uncoiling action, he can temporarily slow or halt the rusher's momentum. As the uncoil is initiated, the legs and hips thrust at an angle toward the rusher's charge. As contact is about to be made, the head, shoulders and arms dip only slightly. Immediately, the back, shoulders, arms and head strike up and through the rusher.

The Recoil Technique

Once the blocker strikes a blow into the rusher, he automatically recoils back to the original football position. The purpose of the first blow was to slow and/or control the defender. Recoiling enables the linemen to stay clear of any defensive pass rush technique of grabbing, hitting, or attempting to turn the blocker. As the blocker returns to a good and low football position, he will again begin similar recoiling attack techniques. This may have to be accomplished three or four times, depending on when the ball is released. In all instances, the blocker should be situated inside forcing the pass rusher outside.

The Ride Technique

The ride technique is initiated after the first blow is struck. Instead of recoiling away from the defensive lineman, however, the blocker remains in contact with him. He must stand and engage with the rusher, and use all of his strength and muscle to ride him outside and away from the quarterback. He must, at all times, maintain a wide base and never cross his feet. His body stays between the defender and the quarterback. If the rush forces outside, the blocker's head slides in that direction. If a stunt pressures inside, the blocker's head shifts inside. If this occurs, the blocker drives the pass rusher forcibly across the passing lane, and continues with him until the ball is thrown.

A Combination of the Recoil and Ride

Both the recoil and ride techniques can be employed at the same time. For example, as the blocker shuffles back and the defender initiates the rush, the lineman can begin the recoil technique. If, after two recoils, he has not halted the momentum, the offensive blocker can instantly employ the ride method.

Substitute and modified blocking techniques should be contrived. On one play, the blocker can use the recoil technique and at the next instant utilize the ride. In other cases, he can be aggressive blocking at the snap of the football, and then promptly drop back, prepared to recoil or ride the defensive lineman.

"Chopping" the Pass Rusher

If all techniques fail to halt the defensive lineman's charge, "chopping" the rusher down at his feet may have to be executed. This does not have to result unless everything else is unsuccessful. The offensive lineman can knock the defender's legs out from under him at any instant during the play. The best opportunity to employ the chop is when the defender is overly aggressive and charging at utmost speed for the quarterback. As the defensive lineman pressures forward, the blocker aims his head and shoulder at the knees and rolls his body into him. This will force the defender to trip and bowl over. Once this is accomplished, the blocker should spring to his feet and be prepared to strike the pass rusher again if he gets up.

SUCCESSFUL PATTERNS WITH FLARE CONTROL

There are many dropback patterns that can be executed with good success. The following (Diagrams 7-8 through 7-10) are two man routes to the strength of the formation with flare control rules employed. Reading adjustments with the pattern are shown where applicable. Changing of routes, as discussed in Chapter 6, is not indicated, but can be installed if desired.

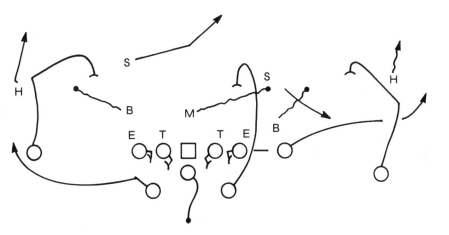

Diagram 7-8

The indicated pattern is the flanker curling and the tight end sprinting to the flat. The flanker breaks his curl and reads the movements of the outside linebacker in the Pro-4. The tight end notices the invert, tries to sprint away from him, and turns upfield. The right halfback keys his flare control assignment. Since the linebacker drops off the line, the halfback runs his required route. The middle linebacker drives past, so he stops and hooks over the middle area. The quarterback's first responsibility is the curl route. If the curl is not open, the passer first scans to the tight end and then the flare back. The offside mongrel route is the curl. The offside halfback swings, hoping to force the weakside linebacker outside to cover him and free the backside curl route.

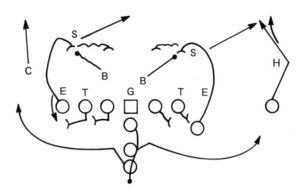

Diagram 7-9

The quarterback signifies for the wide end to run a post and the slot back to execute a hook. The split end, after initiating his cut inside, looks to the offside revolving safety man. If the safety is drifting over to cover the post, the split end will adjust his route more upfield. The slot back releases and hooks while reading the inside linebacker. The fullback keys his linebacker, and since the slot back is routed inside, he swings outside. The backside end's route remains the curl since no other route was indicated for him. The tailback keys his proper linebacker and swings outside and away from the curl.

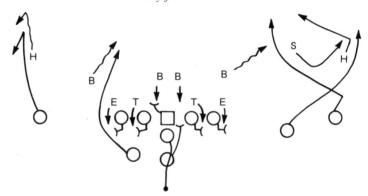

Diagram 7-10

Again, the quarterback called his main pattern to the frontside (split end-delay and flanker-up). However, he changed the backside pattern to an out. The flanker and split end execute their patterns with the end driving underneath and behind the flanker. Since man-to-man is used, the split end attempts to run away from the defensive halfback. However, he must adjust his route because of the outside linebacker's drop. The fullback blocks the linebacker blitz and cannot release. The left halfback, after noticing no rush, releases inside, since the backside split end is running out. The quarterback glances frontside for an opening, and then scans backside.

THREE MAN PATTERNS

A three man pattern (Diagram 7-11) can be called toward the front-side of a formation. Flare control on the frontside does not exist since the halfback releases into the pattern. The backside halfback utilizes flare control while the backside end executes his mongrel route, unless told differently by the quarterback. Line rules will be adjusted slightly. The quarterback play description can be coined in any manner. For example, he can add the number "3" in front of "dropback" indicating a three man dropback pass. Also, three will indicate to the linemen the rule changes necessary to block stunts. A pattern called, therefore, can comprise "3-Dropback, Y-Post, Z-In, Back-swing."

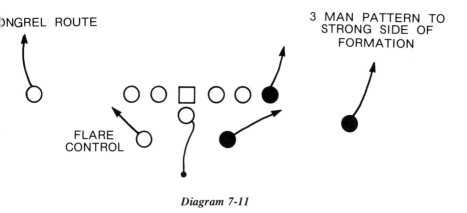

Diagram 7-11

Line Rules

Adequate blocking must be provided for the quarterback. The offense must block any stunt that occurs, especially to the backside. Since a back is automatically releasing, there are only six blockers versus possibly seven or eight rushers. If a defender cannot be blocked, he must come from the frontside, so the quarterback notices him while watching the pattern develop. The rules for the line are as follows, with Diagram 7-12 furnishing offensive blocking patterns.

1. Tackles—Block the #2 Man on the Line of Scrimmage
2. Guards—Block the #1 Man on the Line of Scrimmage
3. Center—Block Over, Linebacker Frontside, Check Backside

1. Tackles   2. Guards

Both the tackles' and guards' rules remain similar to the two man dropback pass. The 5-4 defense, however, forces a change or coaching point. In this case, the frontside tackle blocks the number 1 man, while the guard checks the frontside linebacker and then protects frontside.

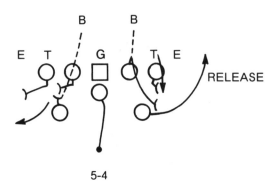

5-4

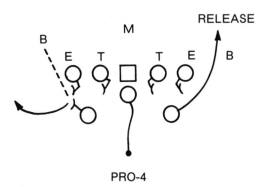

PRO-4

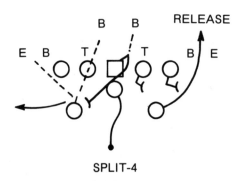

SPLIT-4

Diagram 7-12

3. The Center

There is a modification to the center's rule. He automatically blocks the defensive linemen stationed over him. If there is no one there, however, the center checks the frontside linebacker and immediately shuffles to the backside of the pattern.

The Backside Halfback

The backside halfback keys the first linebacker from the center's position-out. If the defender does not blitz, the halfback will check outside his tackle for any additional rushers. If none show, he will release on his designated flare control route.

SUCCESSFUL THREE MAN PATTERNS

The following patterns (Diagrams 7-13 and 7-14) are three man designated release patterns to the onside of the formation. The backside utilizes flare control principles. Adjustment of patterns is indicated. The blocking just described is illustrated also.

THE STRONG-SIDE "HOT" RECEIVER CONCEPT

Reading and keying before and after the snap of the football was clearly explained and illustrated in Chapter 6. However, an entire picture of the keys and reads from a dropback standpoint was not presented. A three man pattern with keys, reads, adjustments, and possible changing of routes is shown in Diagram 7-15. Line blocking is similar to the two man pattern, with the blockers not responsible for the first linebacker on the frontside of the formation.

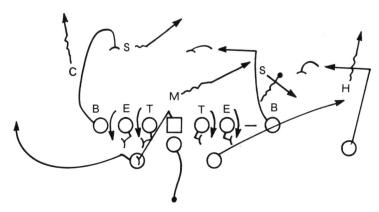

Diagram 7-13

The flanker and tight end are signified to execute a square-in, while the back is designated to run a flat course. The flanker, observing zone coverage, decelerates and locates the vacated areas. The tight end does the same. The onside back releases to the flat and has the option to turn upfield. The backside end does a curl, and the backside halfback, noticing no rush, swings outside.

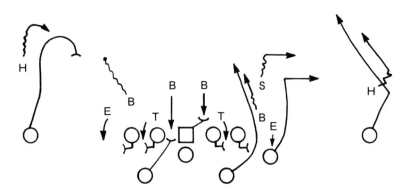

Diagram 7-14

A stunt is used by the Split-4 defense. Since man-to-man is observed, the receivers attempt to outrun their defenders. A good mismatch is the halfback being covered by the linebacker. Since the offside linebacker rushes, the backside halfback remains in to block. The mongrel route is utilized by the split end unless he is told otherwise.

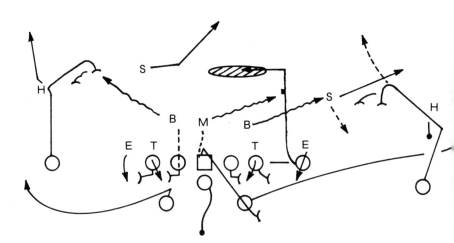

Diagram 7-15

The tight end is the "Hot" receiver in the pattern shown. As the quarterback begins to drop back, he keys the frontside defensive linebacker. If he rushes, the quarterback automatically throws the football to the tight end moving upfield. The tight end releases and keys the same linebacker. If he stunts, the end automatically screams "Hot-Hot" to alert the quarterback of the stunt.
If the stunt does not occur, the quarterback adjusts his key to the strongside safety. If the safety comes forward, as if to invert, the quarterback expects the flanker to execute a post. If the strong-side

safety rotates, then the flanker curls. The flanker adjusts his route on the move also. This will be accomplished whether he changes his route or not.

Once the tight end observes that a stunt does not occur, he executes a square in toward the middle of the field, and reads the linebacker reactions. He will adjust his route accordingly. The halfback releases to the flat and reads the coverage also. If the defenders "hang" to the rear of the flat, the halfback will run shallow to the line, staying away from the defensive halfback or safety. If, however, the defenders react quickly up to the front of the flat, the halfback will turn upfield and scan for any opening between the flat defender and the halfback or safety responsible for the deep outside 1/3 of the field.

The offside end executes his curl route, and adjusts inside or outside according to the play of the linebacker. The offside back keys his assignment and blocks him should he blitz. If he does not stunt, the halfback releases on his swing course. The quarterback scans from the onside to the offside, reading both the defensive moves and the offensive reactions as well.

8

The Weak-Side Dropback Attack
in a High-Scoring Offense

The dropback passing game must be prepared strategically to attack toward the weak side of a formation for a number of reasons. In some cases, the offside end (split end) can be the best receiver on the team. Any backs releasing may be quicker and faster compared to a tight end from the strong side. The defense, also, may prepare its coverages to the strength of the formation because of the two quick receivers' alignment. When this occurs, the offense should take advantage and designate patterns to the weak side, hoping to confuse, deceive, or outwit the defense.

There are numerous methods to attack the weak side from the dropback passing attack. The offense can release one, two or even three receivers to that side (Diagram 8-1). Also, backfield actions can be used to force defensive coverages to the strategical advantage of the offense. Variations of formations can be utilized, including shifting, moving and motioning backs. Whatever the pattern signaled from the backside, the line must modify its blocking rules depending upon the number of backs released. The "hot" receiver principle is another way to attack the weak side.

ATTACKING WITH ONE RECEIVER TO THE WEAK SIDE

If the split end is talented, the offense should attempt to gain a one on one situation for him. While flare control assists the end's route, the offense can utilize other methods to isolate the end. This can be done by setting a strong formation, moving or shifting away from the backside, or sending motion away. Diagrams 8-2 and 8-3 illustrate both motion and an offensive formation

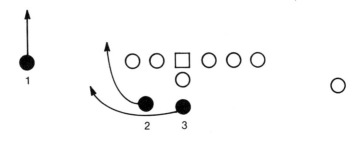

Diagram 8-1

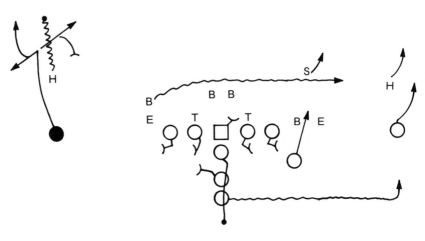

Diagram 8-2

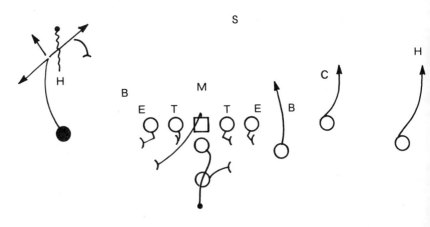

Diagram 8-3

situated strong. Motion is indicated against man-to-man coverage, although similar reaction can occur with zone. The backside linebacker keys and shuffles with the halfback across the field, leaving the split end isolated versus the defensive halfback. Any number of routes can be adopted, both inside and outside, short or deep. In the second diagram, the formation aligns three quick receivers toward one side of the field. The defense reacts by rotating the four spoke secondary. This also provides some field space to operate for the backside end versus one defensive halfback. Again, any route can originate depending upon the situation and the abilities of the split end and defender.

ATTACKING WITH TWO RECEIVERS
TOWARD THE WEAK SIDE

The quarterback can designate two receivers (end and halfback located in the backfield) to quickly release toward the weak side. This automatically becomes the onside of the play, even though the formation is set in the other direction. The quarterback can call "Weak Dropback, X-Square-out, Backhook." This immediately alerts the offense to the side of the formation and the routes to execute. Flare control is utilized, but in a different manner. Since one back releases, another player must assume his assignment. The responsibility of the flare control, therefore, is acquired by the tight end or any player located in his position (slot back).

Flare Control Rules

Diagrams 8-4 and 8-5 illustrate the flare control concept. The fullback is assigned the first linebacker from the center's position-out. If the linebacker stunts, the fullback blocks him. If, however, the linebacker drops into pass coverage, the fullback executes the flare route inside or outside according to the pattern designated. The tight end, in this case, keys the corner area. If two defenders rush outside his offensive tackle, he blocks the widest blitzer. However, if only one man rushes, he releases upfield on his controlled flare route. A hook pattern is executed approximately ten yards upfield. He should

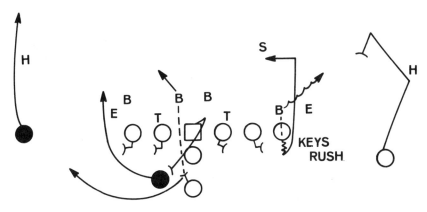

Diagram 8-4
No Rush with Flare Control Routes

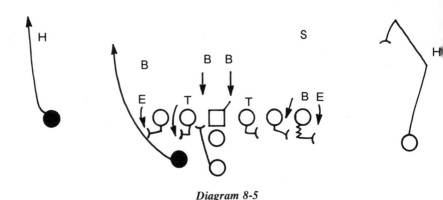

Diagram 8-5
Rush with No Flare Routes

be prepared to slide inside or outside according to the underneath coverage of the defensive scheme.

Line Rules

The line rules remain similar as described for the two man patterns toward the strong side of the formation. The tackles block the number 2 men on the line of scrimmage, while the guards block the number 1 men. The center's rule remains the same, including protecting the frontside of the pattern. One coaching point does prevail. The offside linemen away from the pattern must block straight versus the 5-4 Defense, as explained with a three man pattern to the strong side. The guard first keys the linebacker and then checks backside. The tackle blocks the first down lineman to his side. Diagram 8-6 illustrates the blocking combination versus the 5-4, Pro-4 and Wide Tackle-6 Defenses.

Backside Mongrel Route

When a pattern was indicated to the strong side of a formation, the backside end ran a route already designated for him. Unless told otherwise, he would continue to execute that route. This same concept applies to the backside flanker situated away from the pattern called. Any route can be designated for him. This includes a curl, square-out, square-in, post, etc. If the curl is indicated, he continues to execute it until the quarterback alerts him otherwise. While he is not the primary receiver, it is essential for him to run the curl properly. If the quarterback cannot find a receiver free toward the primary side, he will quickly scan across the field for any other openings. Therefore, it is significant that the flanker read coverages and adjust the curl when necessary.

SUCCESSFUL TWO MAN PATTERNS TO THE WEAK SIDE

Diagram 8-7 illustrates a medium depth pattern with flare control by the fullback and tight end. Diagram 8-8 indicates an up route for the split end and

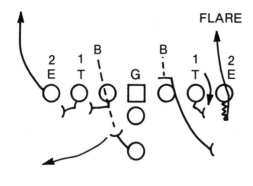

5-4 Defense

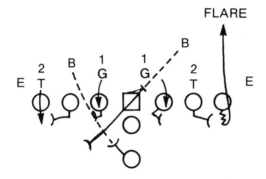

Wide-6 Defense

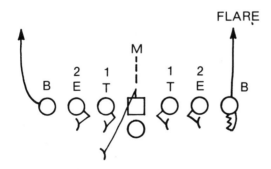

Pro-4 Defense

Diagram 8-6

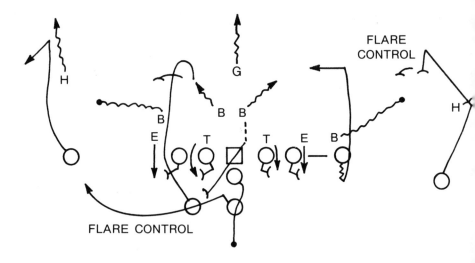

Diagram 8-7

*A square-out is performed by the split-end while a hook-in is done
by the halfback. Both routes can be adjusted, depending upon the
defensive reactions and coverages. The fullback steps left to avoid
the quarterback and keys his linebacker. Since the linebacker
reacted backwards, the fullback swings outside. The tight end sets
back and reads the outside linebacker. Since he is not rushing the
end releases upfield, squares-in approximately at ten yards, and
reads the linebacker responsible for him. The backside flanker
utilizes a curl and reacts in or out, depending upon the outside
linebacker's coverage. As the quarterback retreats, he scans first
to the split end and second to the halfback. The fullback or split
receiver should be open since one zone is flooded by two receivers.
If these receivers are not clear, however, he will glance backside
for the tight end or flanker.*

a square-out by the tailback. Flare control assignments are executed by the
fullback and slot back.

ATTACKING WITH TWO RECEIVERS, BUT FORCING ROTATION AWAY

With the dropback passing game, many defenses key the fullback and
rotate in the direction he goes. This is applied mainly by four deep secondaries. When coverages are geared in this manner, the offense can foresee and
direct the defensive coverage away from the onside pattern. The fullback
simply steps in the direction of the formation or opposite the designated
pattern. Of course, flare control routes will alter. When this is accomplished,
a three man release to the weak side will never occur. However, from an
offensive standpoint, more will be gained. Blocking rules are also modified

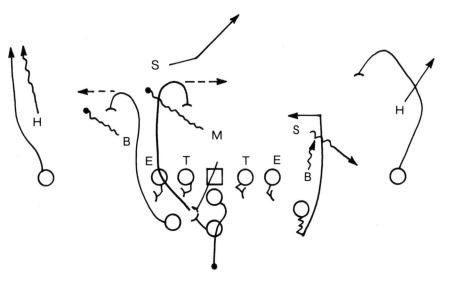

Diagram 8-8

An up and out pattern is demonstrated with the split end and halfback. The fullback executes his flare control route and reads the middle linebacker for coverage. Since the middle linebacker overruns outside, the fullback hooks inside. If man-to-man is shown, the fullback continues inside on a square-in route. In many cases the middle linebacker would be flowing in the opposite direction, causing a more easily completed pattern. Both the slot back and offside split end operate their required routes.

slightly. The greatest advantage of this offensive attack is that it usually forces secondaries to rotate away from the intended pattern. Also, linebackers are sent opposite the area of attack. Diagram 8-9 illustrates this passing strategy versus a Pro-4 Defense. As can be seen, the split end and halfback have less defenders to cover them. The defensive halfback is revolving back to the deep outside 1/3, and the only defender underneath is the outside linebacker.

Line Rules and Flare Control

There are a few modifications necessary with this strategical attack. The fullback and the offensive center switch assignments. The center keys the linebacker to the patterns onside. He shuffles out and to the onside as he did before, if his responsibility did not blitz. The fullback keys the first linebacker away from the pattern designated. His rule is exactly like the two man pattern employed with the strong-side dropback game. If the linebacker does not stunt, the fullback releases on his flare control route. This time, however, it is away from the particular pattern signified. His assignment is to force the defensive linebackers and halfbacks to conclude that the basic pattern is

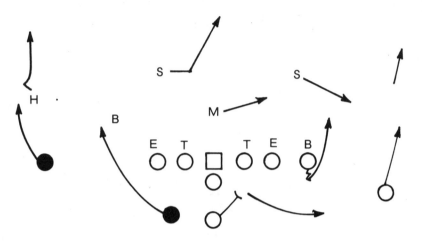

Diagram 8-9

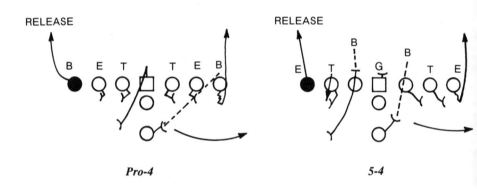

Pro-4   *5-4*

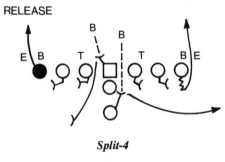

Split-4

Diagram 8-10
Onside is Left

toward the formation strength. Diagram 8-10 illustrates the blocking patterns and flare control used by both the fullback and tight end (slot back).

SUCCESSFUL TWO MAN PATTERNS WITH FLARE CONTROL ROUTES DIVERTED AWAY

Diagrams 8-11 and 8-12 illustrate the advantages of this false key system versus the 5-4 and Pro-4 Defenses. In both instances, defensive coverage is forced away from the main pattern. If a stunt occurs the quarterback will have maximum coverage to his backside. While a strong onside rush creates pressure he can easily see it and react to his receivers accordingly. The backside pattern can also be altered by the quarterback if he thinks it's necessary.

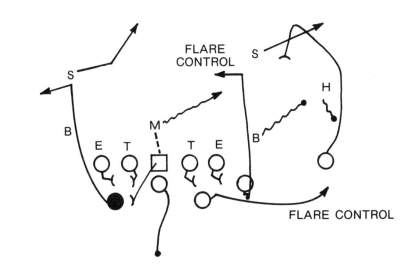

Diagram 8-11
Versus the Pro-4

The split end and halfback execute square-out routes versus the outside linebacker and defensive halfback. The middle linebacker, however, is drawn away by the three man release toward the strength of the formation. The quarterback sets and looks to the onside pattern first. Adjustments of the routes can result if different coverages are seen. Openings should easily occur. If they do not, however, the quarterback can scan to the flare control and curl routes.

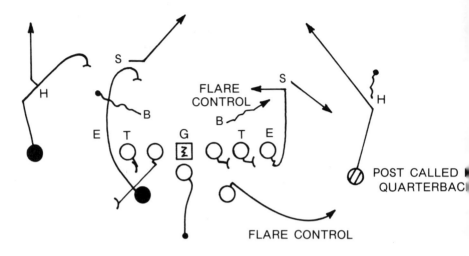

Diagram 8-12

A curl and hook pattern is designated weak side. A post route offside is utilized by the quarterback as a variation. Flare routes are demonstrated by the right halfback and tight end. Reading and keying for route adjustments can also be realized.

ATTACKING WITH THREE RECEIVERS
TOWARD THE WEAK SIDE

Three receivers (an end and two backs) can release to the formation weak side. Since there are only six blockers available (if a wide-out to the offside is used), and all backs release, flare control can not occur. Line rules are modified so protection is more effective. Diagram 8-13 illustrates the three man release. A wing formation can also be used for maximum protection on the backside. The advantage of this attack is the releasing of three men weak-side, even though stunting can occur.

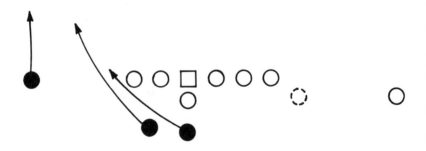

Diagram 8-13

Line Rules and Possible Flare Control

Since four receivers are releasing from the line and backfield, only six blockers remain protecting the quarterback. It is conceivable the defense could rush seven or eight defenders. If this occurs, however, the rush should come from the side the quarterback is throwing so that he can notice both his receivers and the rush. Maximum protection on the backside should be achieved. Area blocking is the rule. The backside end, tackle, guard, and center set in their respective areas and block any defender rushing over them. If a rush is not forthcoming, each blocker will shuffle backside for other defenders, or assist with another blocker on a defensive lineman. Possible flare control can be adopted by the tight end. If his man drops into coverage, he can release. The frontside guard and tackle area block also. However, if a rush does not occur over their area, they will shuffle outside (frontside) and block. Diagram 8-14 illustrates blocking versus the Split-4, 5-4, and Pro-4 defensive schemes.

FLARE CONTROL

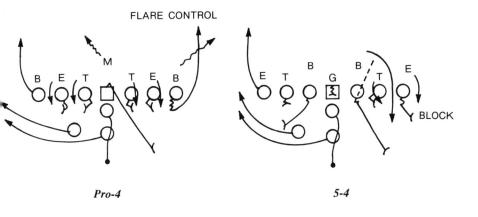

Pro-4   *5-4*

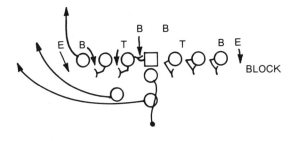

Split-4
Diagram 8-14

SUCCESSFUL THREE MAN PATTERNS TO THE WEAK SIDE

Three man backside routes can be designed similar to the two man patterns with flare control exercised. Any number of patterns can be used, including short, medium, long, and delay looks. Diagram 8-15 indicates the split end driving in a post route, while the halfback hooks and the fullback swings outside. The backside flanker executes a basic route (in this case a square-out) unless directed otherwise by the quarterback.

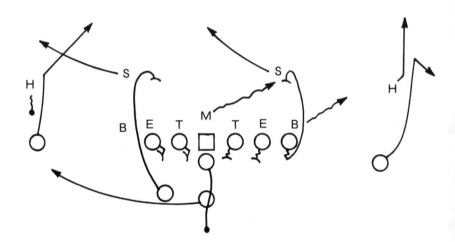

Diagram 8-15

The quarterback drops back and scans the three man pattern im-mediately. In this fashion, he can read any rush occurring. The split end does a post route and attempts to run away from the revolving defensive safety. The halfback executes a hook and keys the inside linebacker. Since the middle linebacker covers the back-side tight end's flare route, he just halts and waits. The fullback swings outside, gaining depth, so he attains some maneuverable area if the ball is thrown to him. The backside tight end can flare because of the outside linebacker's drop coverage. He reads and keys as did the onside halfback. The flanker executes a square-out. If the middle linebacker covered the frontside pattern and every receiver was covered (the defense guessed right), the quarterback should look to the flare control tight end or flankerback's route.

THE WEAK-SIDE HOT RECEIVER CONCEPT

The principle of a hot receiver can be employed toward the weak side of a formation. Two or three man routes can be developed. Diagram 8-16 is an example of a two man pattern called to the split end. The offside tight end and flanker apply backside routes, while the right halfback uses flare control principles. Three receivers can be sent toward the formation's weak side, with the hot receiver concept also utilized (Diagram 8-17). In this instance, the backside slot halfback keys for flare control.

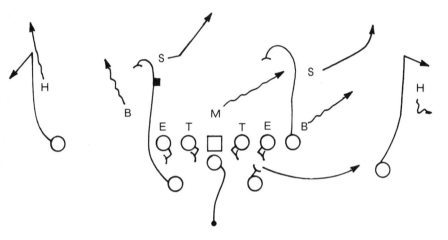

Diagram 8-16

The dropback action with the flow of the right halfback (fullback) forces the defensive secondary to rotate away from the main pattern. The split end squares out. The left halfback maneuvers up-field as shown, and keys the middle linebacker (any inside linebacker) for a stunt. If the linebacker stunts forward toward the quarterback, he yells "hot-hot." The quarterback keys the linebacker also, and will throw the ball if a blitz occurs. In this case the linebacker sprints away, so the basic pattern with the split end and left halfback is covered by only one defender (the outside linebacker). The flanker and tight end can run any route. The right halfback (fullback) utilizes flare control principles. The quarterback looks immediately to the split end. If the outside linebacker falls underneath, the quarterback glances to the left halfback. If he is covered, the quarterback will scan across field for other outlet receivers (tight end, flanker, or right halfback).

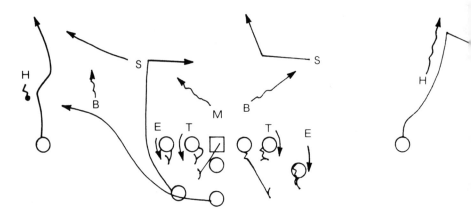

Diagram 8-17

As illustrated, the hot receiver is the left halfback. If the middle linebacker blitzes, the ball will be delivered by the quarterback. The split end is on a flag course, while the fullback drives into the flat. The backside slot halfback remains in and blocks because of the rush. The backside flanker squares out. The quarterback can signify an alternate route for him if necessary. The three man pattern is easily executed because maximum protection is employed along the line of scrimmage.

9

The Sprint (Roll)-Out Pass Attack

The sprint or roll-out passing game attempts to attain outside position on the defensive end and attack the defensive corner or flat. Usually the block of the fullback is initiated against the end, although halfbacks can be so instructed also. The quarterback's fundamentals and techniques of the sprint and roll-out action are vividly described and photographed in Chapter 1. The theory of this attack desires to create pressure in one specific area of the defensive scheme. In this instance, the attack focuses on the outside swing, short flat, and the vertical outside areas of the defensive secondary. The quarterback has the opportunity to run with the ball, which can apply additional pressure for the defense also. Diagram 9-1 illustrates the sprint or roll-out attack versus the various outside areas of the defensive secondary. The routes and patterns adopted should be geared to these specific areas indicated. With the quarterback forceably on the move he does not have the vision or the physical attributes to pass the ball toward the middle or, for that matter, across field in the opposite direction.

THE STRENGTHS AND ADVANTAGES OF THE
SPRINT (ROLL)—OUT PASSING ATTACK

The strengths and advantages of both the sprint or roll-out passing games are as follows:

1. A quarterback who is an average passer or does not possess the capability to throw the ball over a wide range of the field can adopt this form of attack.
2. Losing yardage is minimized. The passer is continually running toward the line of scrimmage.

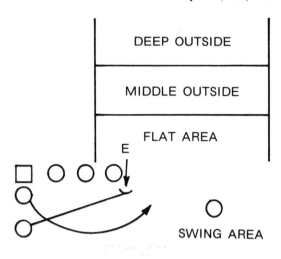

Diagram 9-1

3. The pass routes executed by the receivers are in direct line and view of the quarterback.

4. The sprint and roll-out pass easily coordinates with other plays in an offense, including the belly series, veer series, wishbone, counters, etc.

5. It creates an easy read for the passer. Through constant practice, he can develop proficiency regarding when to pass and when to run.

6. The possibility of a pass on every down causes the secondary defenders to hold or freeze in their positions while deciding whether it is a run or pass.

7. While the defense may attempt to apply internal pressure through the employment of blitzing or stunting, the quarterback is constantly clearing away from the intended rush.

8. Persistent pressure is placed on the defensive halfback or cornerman because they have to defend against the run or pass.

9. Since half of the defensive linemen must chase the passer farther, limited pressure is created against him from the outside. A longer rush, therefore, is needed for the defense. This creates a physical toll for the defenders.

10. The offensive linemen have easier and better blocking assignments since the defensive linemen have only one direction ro rush the quarterback.

11. The defensive secondary must utilize different coverages whenever the quarterback moves in a sprint or roll-out fashion, causing additional problems for them.

12. The running attack is greatly expanded since the quarterback is now a runner.

PASS ROUTES AND PATTERNS

The pass routes and patterns adopted by the sprint-out game are somewhat more diversified than the dropback passing game. Since the quarterback is focusing on a particular area of the field, the receiver routes must be executed in that direction. When a receiver is aligned tight in an offensive set, his routes will be geared outside. If, however, he is stationed wide, the routes will be either inside (no more than a few steps) or outside. This also will depend upon the availability of field space, formations, timing of the pattern, etc. Diagram 9-2 indicates a pro-flanker formation, with the tight end aiming his patterns outside and the flanker running inside or outside. While the pattern called is very significant, the formations and the alignment of receivers are vital factors in the success of the play also.

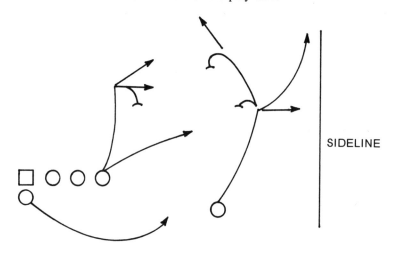

SIDELINE

Diagram 9-2

As can be seen by the diagram, the tight end should not execute a route toward the middle of the formation, since he would be completely out of the quarterback's view. His routes, therefore, can be a short flat, square-out, flag, hook out, flat and up, etc. The outside receiver can maneuver in any direction, since he is located wide and the quarterback is sprinting toward him. His routes, therefore, can be a square-out, square-in, hook in or out, post, curl, flag, up, etc. Intelligent and strategical planning with the various pass patterns should be developed. Patterns will vary according to the many pass defensive coverages, offensive formations, motion, receivers, the quarterback's ability, etc.

READING COVERAGES

As was discussed quite extensively in Chapter 6, the reading and keying of defensive coverages can be adopted with the sprint or roll-out game.

Recognizing whether the defense is operating man-to-man, zone, or a combination coverage has to be accomplished while running. The quarterback is not setting up and scanning the field, as designed with the dropback game. He is continually sprinting toward the area of the pass pattern and trying to pick out his best receiver. The receivers should also read defenses. Proper drilling, timing, and coordination must be achieved if success is to be attained by reading.

FORMATION UTILIZATION

Unlike the dropback pass, the sprint or roll-out game can utilize various formations. Width is not necessary, but can easily be adopted. A typical wing formation is an example. While the dropback pass does not use it, the sprint out pass will. The wingback can drive to the flat while the tight end releases on a flag route. The quarterback is running in their direction, which makes it a very simple and basic pattern to execute (Diagram 9-3).

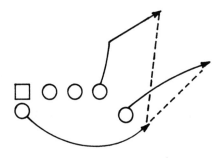

Diagram 9-3

Various widths of flankers and split ends can also be utilized. This spreads the defensive alignment and provides the wide-out the opportunity to execute routes both inside and outside. The inside receiver can release to any area also, but has more of a tendency to run some form of an out pattern. Motion by an offensive back can be installed to gain width, force the defense to react before the snap of the ball, and possibly create weaknesses in the defense.

SPRINT (ROLL)—OUT BLOCKING ASSIGNMENTS

Since the quarterback is continually removing himself from the inside, the blocking by the linemen and backs is quite different than the dropback scheme. The essential blockers for the sprint-out game are the interior linemen and the fullback. In most instances, the fullback is employed to block with the halfbacks releasing into the pattern. However, there are times when halfbacks block and the fullback releases. Many teams use both the fullback and halfback to block, which greatly enhances success of the play.

Line Blocking

Line blocking rules are indicated, with proper execution and coaching points explained. Diagram 9-4 illustrates the various blocks versus the defenses.

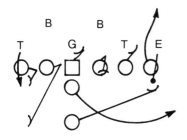

Versus the 5-4

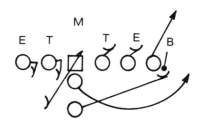

Versus the Pro-4

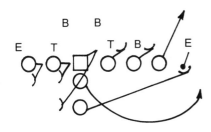

Versus the Split-4

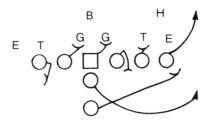

Versus the 6-5 Goal Line

Diagram 9-4
Sprint or Roll-Out Blocking Versus Various Defenses

Onside Tackle

The rule of the onside tackle is to block the first defensive lineman on or to the outside of him. On the snap of the football the tackle aims his head for the outside hip of his defensive opponent. A lead step is initiated in that direction. He remains low and places his head in the defender's outside knee to scramble block him. At this point, the tackle continues to scramble him by keeping his hands and feet moving. If the tackle falls to the ground, he must work himself up and run with the defender. The onside tackle should never allow the rusher to gain penetration into the backfield. The quarterback's route is outside at a certain depth. If penetration occurs, it will alter his course, which will definitely disrupt the timing and success of the pass pattern.

Onside Guard

The rule of the onside guard is to block the Number 1 defender counting from the center out. The onside guard's primary responsibility is similar to the onside tackle's. He must fire out low and aggressive to make it look like a run. He aims his head for the outside hip of the opponent and executes a scramble block. If a linebacker is aligned directly over him, the guard initiates a short jab step with his inside leg and keys the movement of the linebacker. If he stunts, the guard blocks him. However, if the linebacker flows into pass defense, the guard will assist other blockers in the immediate area.

Center

The center's rule for the sprint-out is to block the Number 0 man. In many cases a Number 0 man is not present. He should alert the onside guard, therefore, as to who Number 0 is so the guard can block the Number 1 man. The center's assignment is similar to the onside guard's. If he is covered, he strikes a blow on the outside hip of the defender and scramble blocks him. If he is not covered he drops back in a good cup formation protection. He should continue to use a wide foot base, with hips bent, back straight, and the head up. His feet are moving at all times scanning for any defenders seeping through his area of responsibility. If there are no defenders rushing, he immediately shuffles outside and blocks any defender rushing from that area.

Offside Guard

The offside guard's rule is to block the Number 1 defender. He applies cup or dropback blocking techniques. Aggressive fire-out is not essential, since the quarterback is sprinting away from both the offside guard's and tackle's position. At the snap of the football, the offside guard pushes away with the inside foot and begins to use proper dropback blocking technique. He maintains a wide base with the feet in motion. An attempt should be made to force the opponent away and to the outside of the pass lane. If the Number 1 man is a linebacker, he first checks the rush. If a stunt does not occur, the guard turns outside and is prepared to block other defenders or the defensive end.

Offside Tackle

The offside tackle's rule is to block the Number 2 rusher. He should apply fundamentals and techniques similar to those of the offside guard. If a defender does not rush (linebacker), the tackle can shuffle outside for the defensive end.

Fullback

The fullback's block becomes very important. He must block the defensive end so the quarterback has the opportunity to continue on the outside path. If the block by the fullback fails, the quarterback has to pull up. The quarterback's passing lane is quite different when he cannot get outside and thus does not create pressure on the corner for the run either.

The fullback's rule is to block the first defender outside the onside tackle's position. On the snap of the football, the fullback executes a lead step and aims for a spot one foot wider than the tight end's alignment. His course is straight and should not be in any way a looped or circled path. As he reaches the defensive end, the fullback aims his head on the end's outside knee and attempts to force him inside and knock him down. The fullback situates his legs underneath him. He should not throw the block quickly so as to lose his balance and fall to the ground. It is essential that the fullback command a clear and direct path toward the defensive end. If the path is wide and the end crashes on a stunt inside, it may be difficult for the fullback to block him.

ATTACKING WITH ONE RECEIVER

One receiver can be used with the sprint-out pass. In most cases this will be an end. He can be aligned in any position, but is best when he is split from the formation. In this manner, the split end has the ability to perform a number of pass routes versus the defensive halfback. These routes can be signified in the huddle, read on the line before the snap of the football, or read after the ball has been put into play. Diagram 9-5 illustrates a one man release. Throwing to one receiver should result when the receiver is single covered by a defensive halfback. If there is more than one defender stationed in proximity to the split receiver, sprinting to him is not advisable. An extra receiver would then be necessary to clear pass lanes or be installed as a primary target.

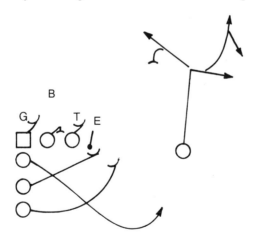

Diagram 9-5

ATTACKING WITH TWO RECEIVERS

The most common form of attack is the utilization of two pass receivers. They can be situated in any alignment desired. There must be, however, a purpose for the various widths adopted. Formation receiver alignment will be dependent upon the pattern executed, the opponent's defensive scheme and the amount of field space allotted (hash marks, middle of the field, etc.).

The most common sprint-out pass is illustrated in Diagram 9-6. The wing back releases to the flat area while the tight end runs a flag route. The blocking is indicated with the quarterback sprinting outside and locating the open receiver. The offside end and halfback execute their backside or throwback pattern, which is explained in the following chapter. A similar pattern is illustrated in Diagram 9-7 to the split end side. In this case, the split end and halfback execute the pattern called, while the tight end and wing back exercise their throwback pattern.

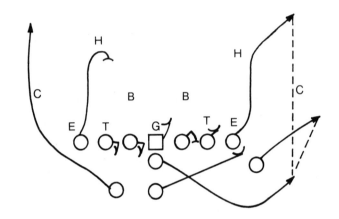

Diagram 9-6

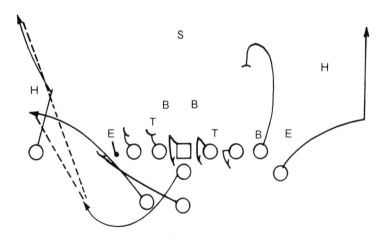

Diagram 9-7

There are many and various other sprint or roll-out patterns that can be included in an offensive attack. Diagrams 9-8 through 9-10 indicate only three examples of different formations and patterns used versus contrasting secondary defenses.

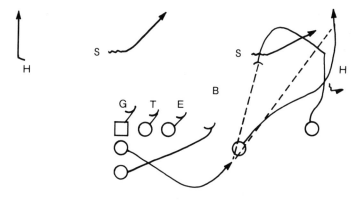

Diagram 9-8

A sprint-out versus a shifted 5-4 Defense performing rotation is shown. The split end runs a curl while the wide slot executes a flat and up route. The quarterback sprints out and first scans to the curl pattern for any open lanes. If he notices the slot open deep, however, he may attempt to pass him immediately.

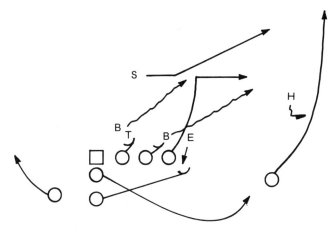

Diagram 9-9

A flanker formation is indicated versus the Split-4 Defense. A three deep rotation is performed as the quarterback rolls out. If the quarterback is reading he will immediately notice that the flanker may be open, due to the defensive safety's position far from the flanker. He realizes zone coverage is occurring and, therefore, the tight end's route and passing lane will be open between the linebackers also.

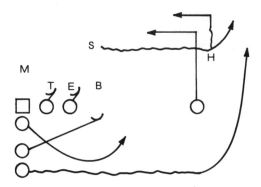

Diagram 9-10

*Motion is indicated versus the Pro-4 Defense. A square-in is exe-
cuted by the split end, while the motion back does an up route.
This is a good pattern whether it is used against zone or man-to-
man. The square-in receiver can either accelerate or slow down
his pace, according to the coverage, and the quarterback should
be able to locate an open lane. The up route can be thrown especially if the receiver has beaten the defender.*

THREE-MAN PASS PATTERNS

Three receivers can also be released into a pattern on one side of the
formation with the sprint-out series. Only specific formations can be used in
order to coordinate the receivers' routes. The quarterback continually attempts
to run outside and create pressure at the corner. Diagrams 9-11 and 9-12
illustrate two examples of three-man patterns.

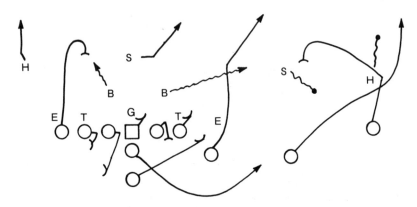

Diagram 9-11

*A three-man pattern is illustrated with the split end executing a
curl, the wide slot an up and the close slot a flag. Reading and
keying by the quarterback and receivers can easily be accomplished.*

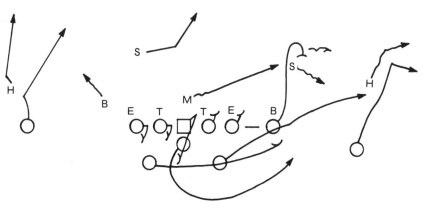

Diagram 9-12

A roll-out from a pro formation. The flanker executes a square-out, while the tight end does a hook and the halfback releases to the flat.

THE SEMI-SPRINT (ROLL)—OUT ATTACK

There are numerous instances when the quarterback does not desire to completely sprint outside the defensive end. One case is when the defensive end penetrates deep and/or wide outside, totally preventing the passer from running outside of him. Specific pass patterns should be designed to attack this defensive maneuver. The semi-sprint or roll attack provides the quarterback an opportunity to begin a sprint action, but to stop on his course directly behind the offensive tackle (Diagram 9-13). He sets at a distance of approximately 5 to 7 yards and automatically scans the pattern called. The advantage of the action is that it allows the quarterback to set up as he would in the dropback game, but it also places him closer to the pattern executed. It forces the defensive secondary to react differently because of the sprint or roll-out look. Secondary coverages and movements can be strategically implemented in order to counter the sprint or roll-out actions. However, at the same time, pass patterns can be designed to better attack the defense, both frontside and backside as well (Chapter 10).

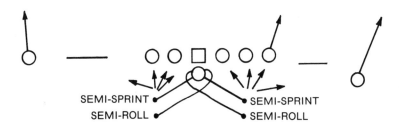

Diagram 9-13

Diagrams 9-14 through 9-16 illustrate the semi-sprint and roll-out series with various pass routes explained. Many other patterns can be adopted according to the defensive schemes and coverage used.

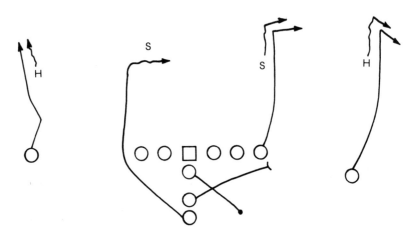

Diagram 9-14

The flanker and tight end both execute square-out routes. This is an excellent pass pattern for the quarterback to read. If the strong-side safety covers the tight end, the flanker should be free. If the flanker is somewhat double covered, then the tight end should be open.

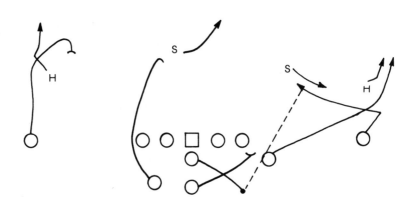

Diagram 9-15

The onside split end releases on a pick route. He attempts to run underneath the slot back's up action. The quarterback pulls up and tries to pass the ball as soon as an open lane occurs. This is accomplished between linebacker and secondary defenders.

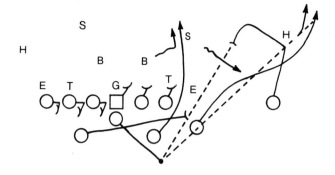

Diagram 9-16

A three-man pass pattern is indicated. The split end runs a curl while the slot releases on an up route. The offensive halfback releases from the backfield and attempts to misdirect linebacker coverage away from the curl receiver.

10

The Sprint (Roll) Back
Pass Attack

The purpose of the sprint or roll back passing game is to strategically and intelligently attack a defensive pass coverage's movement and weaknesses. The sprint back pass is utilized only when the defense reacts to halt the offense's sprint or roll out. The offense continually sprints and rolls in an attempt to get outside the defensive end and create pressure on the corner area. However, when the defense begins to adjust and overly react, the offense should begin to employ the sprint or roll back attack.

WHEN TO SPRINT (ROLL) BACK

The offense should employ the sprint back pass only when certain defensive adjustments exist. The secondary coverages used and the different linebacker reactions should be attacked strategically. Diagrams 10-1 and 10-2 illustrate secondary rotation of the three and four deep defenses. As can be seen, the defensive halfback rotates forward to the flat, while the defensive safety (safeties) and halfback progress to their respective deep areas. After the secondary commits itself, as indicated, the offense has an excellent opportunity to apply the sprint back pass, with specific designed patterns thrown away from the rotation.

Attacking linebacker coverage is also very important. The offense should be prepared to throw back when the linebackers are either quickly reacting to the side of the sprint, are slow reacting to their respected coverage areas, are assigned specific areas toward the side of the quarterback action, and/or rotate deep with the defensive secondary. Diagrams 10-3 through 10-6 indicate these various defensive maneuvers, with the weakness areas shown for the offense to attack.

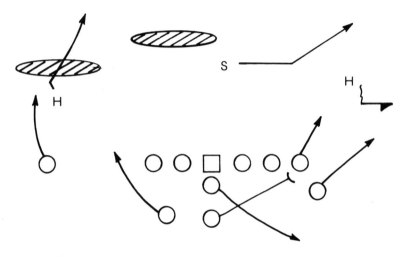

Diagram 10-1
Three Deep Rotation

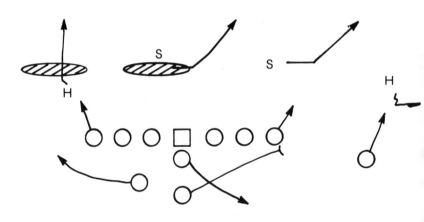

Diagram 10-2
Four Deep Rotation

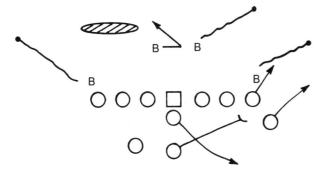

Diagram 10-3
The backside linebacker pursuing quickly and not flowing to his respected hook area.

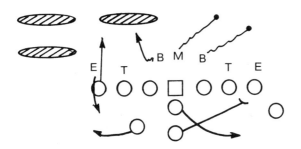

Diagram 10-4
A Tennessee 5-4 linebacker reacting slow to his respected area.

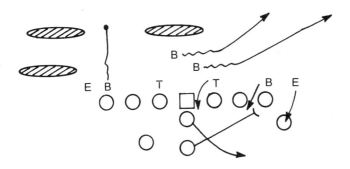

Diagram 10-5
A Split-4 inside linebacker assigned an area to the outside, leaving the backside outside linebacker covering away from the action.

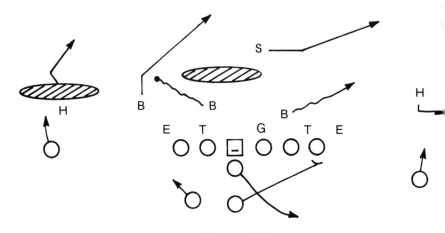

Diagram 10-6
An outside linebacker utilized in the secondary rotation of a three
deep. As can be seen, weakness areas readily unfold.

ATTACKING WITH FORMATIONS

Proper strategy should be adopted with the throwback pass. Patterns to the side of the formation can be successful only when the proper widths and depths of the ends and backs are utilized. Splitting ends and placing offensive backs in certain positions can force defensive adjustments and provide different coverages. If only slight width is obtained, for example, a specific pattern may not find success due to the alignment and play of the defenders. Timing is also essential. A halfback releasing from his regular position is quite different than if he released from the "I" tailback or a slot alignment. Therefore, intelligent formations must be designated by the quarterback when routes and patterns are executed.

ATTACKING KEYS

Most defensive coverages have linebackers and secondary personnel keying offensive backs and ends for their rotation and/or man-to-man assignments. The offense should discover these keys and responsibilities. This can be pinpointed in films, scouting or game observation. A clear example is shown in Diagram 10-7. An "I" formation is illustrated, with the tailback flowing in the direction of the fullback. The offside linebacker shuffles to the frontside of the pattern because of his tailback key. This may open passing lanes that would not exist otherwise for one or possibly two receivers, as indicated on the backside of the sprint. If the tailback went toward the throwback side, he may have brought another defender in the area, forcing the primary receiver (split end) to be covered on his square-in or curl route. Many other examples can be shown also. Intelligent strategy of the throwback pass can be developed, and more success will be the result.

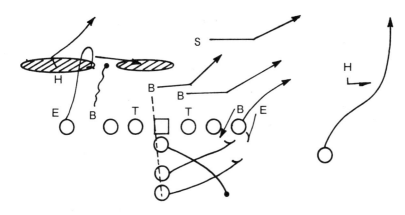

Diagram 10-7

QUARTERBACK TECHNIQUE FOR THE SPRINT (ROLL) BACK

The quarterback initiates a lead step out from the center, just as he did with the sprint out. A reverse pivot is employed if the roll-out technique or action was established in the offense. The quarterback now sprints at the same angle and depth as if circling outside the defensive end. However, as he reaches the point directly behind the offensive tackle, he immediately plants the foot that first propelled him in that direction. If he is sprinting right, the right foot plants—if sprinting left, the left foot halts the forward progression. Once his momentum has stopped, he should be located approximately 5 to 6 yards in depth behind the offensive tackle's position. He is set in a good passing position. His feet are well balanced underneath him, and he is standing tall and scanning downfield in the direction of his sprint or roll action.

It is essential that the throwback position be maintained. He should never be wider than the offensive tackle because good passing lanes and angles to the backside are necessary. At the same time, the blocking is geared to protect behind the tackle's spot. He should get set as quickly as possible so he has time to pass the ball. A few quarterbacks situate either behind the offensive guard or the guard-tackle seam. However, this is not desired. It doesn't furnish the defense a beneficial sprint or roll-out look. Proper drilling and timing is essential if the throwback action is to be successful.

Once the quarterback sets to pass, his eyes are trained toward the side of his sprint. Hopefully, this action forces a defensive consciousness to the frontside. However, once the quarterback knows his pattern is developing backside, he immediately shifts his eyes toward the primary and secondary receivers. If he is keying and reading linebackers or secondary movement, his scan backside may be slightly quicker. Once he notices an opening, he should deliver the football with authority and speed. His pass will be longer than usual at times, because of the throwing distance developed from the sprint action.

THROWBACK BLOCKING

Blocking for the throwback pass is very similar to the sprint or roll-out pass attack. The blocking rules are exactly the same. However, the techniques of each position alter. Since the quarterback is aligned behind the offensive tackle, the line blocks are different. The offensive tackle and guard are continually aggressive on their first inital charge across the line, but then gather up their feet, acquire body control, and begin to block the rushers away and outside of the passer's position. Ride and recoil techniques are used. The center, as well as the backside guard and tackle, are more aggressive since the quarterback is not rolling outside the defensive end. They block their defenders by utilizing ride and recoil techniques, and by driving the defenders away and outside the passer's position.

The fullback's responsibility and assignment is similar to that when the quarterback is sprinting outside the end. He explodes from his position and takes a course at the defensive end as if the quarterback was driving outside. He must show the defensive end this action. If the fullback decelerates or adopts a different angle, the defensive end can "read" this action and know immediately whether the quarterback is maneuvering outside or not. This slight advantage for the defensive end may result in a speedier rush at the quarterback and force him to deliver the ball sooner. It is necessary, therefore, that the fullback show the same angle and thrust at the end. Once he reaches the defensive end, he should attempt to go "through" him. This signifies that he drive his head into the crotch or knee of the end, and continue to run and force him back, outside, and away from the quarterback. If the fullback can knock the defender down, all the better. The fullback's action into the crotch or knee will force the end to bring his hands down and react off the fullback, presenting the quarterback added time to pass.

ATTACKING PATTERNS FROM THE THROWBACK

One or two man routes and patterns are usually thrown with the throwback action. It is significant to emphasize that the throwback is thrown only when the defensive secondary coverage is rotating and the defensive linebackers are reacting to the side of the sprint or roll-out attack. It should be remembered, also, that if linebackers are not reacting to the sprint side on designated patterns and schemes, then openings will occur frontside. Once defensive coverages are geared to stop the sprint-out, the throwback pass should be introduced.

The defense and the coverage used dictate the kind of pass thrown. Certain passes are more successful versus one defense, for example, but not against another. A four deep secondary coverage places defenders in different areas than the three deep, with the linebacker coverages changing also. The coach and quarterback must know and understand the defense employed and attack it properly.

ATTACKING THE THREE DEEP

The three deep coverage usually has four linebackers stationed underneath for the short areas. Once rotation is initiated toward the sprint action, weaknesses will evolve on the backside. This is especially true in the *deep* areas. In most cases two linebackers are designated for the backside, but at times, due to coverage or stunt, there may only be one linebacker. Diagram 10-8 illustrates the weakness areas developed with the throwback pass.

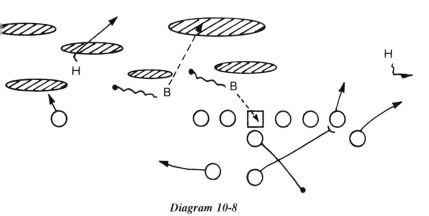

Diagram 10-8

The diagram indicates rotation of the three deep. The backside linebackers are flowing to their respective zone areas. However, one can be assigned to plug through the center, or assist deep on coverage, etc. Added weakness will then result.

There are many imaginative patterns that can be unfolded to attack the eight man front. The offense should immediately attack the deep area where only one defensive halfback is covering. The best method is to send two receivers deep, attempting to force the defender to cover two men. Diagrams 10-9 and 10-10 illustrate simple routes that can place the defensive halfback in an awkward position.

While the deep areas can be exploited, the quarterback and coach should know the defensive execution of the backside linebackers to sprint action. As previously mentioned, some linebackers are assigned for plugging while others are responsible for depth. Whatever the case may be, however, the offense should be prepared to attack the alignments and coverages of these linebackers with well designed and well timed pass patterns. Since two linebackers are usually in the coverage attacking this defensive play will be provided. If there happens to be only one linebacker assigned backside, however, the better it is for the offense.

It is difficult to attack two linebackers, but if the offense can key and read their movements on ball flow, routes can be more successful. Usually, one receiver's responsibility is to misdirect a linebacker out of position. One example is indicated in Diagram 10-11. The right end releases from the line and hooks out and away from the inside linebacker. The offensive halfback is sent to the flat and draws the outside linebacker away from the primary

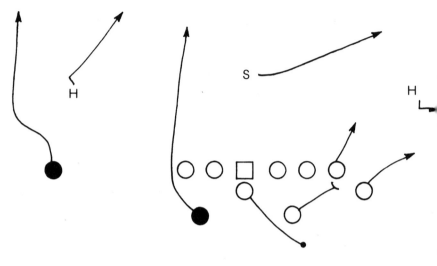

Diagram 10-9

The split end executes an up route while the halfback releases on a streak. The quarterback can now key the defensive halfback and throw to the open receiver.

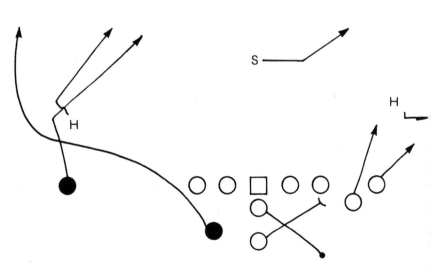

Diagram 10-10

In this case the split end executes a post route while the halfback runs a flat and up. Again, the quarterback keys the defensive halfback for the open receiver.

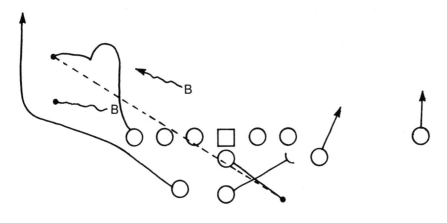

Diagram 10-11

receiver. The quarterback should lead the ball well outside so the inside linebacker does not have an opportunity for an interception.

A few teams utilize linebackers in the deep secondary coverage. The offense can take advantage of this play. First, and foremost, there is only one linebacker available to cover the throwback. This can easily be attacked with two receivers. Another method is for a receiver to key the linebacker responsible for the deep coverage. If the linebacker goes deep, the receiver maneuvers short, and if the defender continues short, the receiver naturally sprints deep. Diagram 10-12 illustrates this point. The outside linebacker, in many

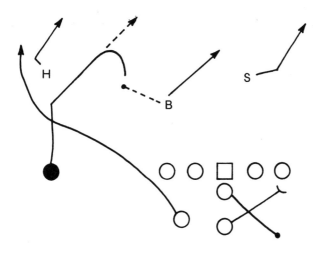

Diagram 10-12

instances, drives for the deep secondary. The split end, as he releases off the snap, keys the movements of the linebacker. If the linebacker drives deep, the end executes a simple curl pattern. However, if the defender remains short, the end breaks the route towards the post. The offensive halfback releases to the flat and attracts any other available linebacker outside. The quarterback keys the linebacker so he recognizes automatically whether the ball is to be thrown short or long.

ATTACKING THE FOUR DEEP

Weakness areas of the four deep defense are slightly different than the three deep secondary. When the four deep rotates towards the sprint or roll-out action, the flat and the three deep areas nearest the play are covered. For a sound pass defense, there are usually three linebackers used underneath for support. One linebacker is always employed for any backside coverage. Diagram 10-13 illustrates the Pro-4 Defensive coverage. As can be seen, the weakness areas are located in the short zones. There are three secondary defenders responsible deep, which creates some difficulties for completing the longer pass.

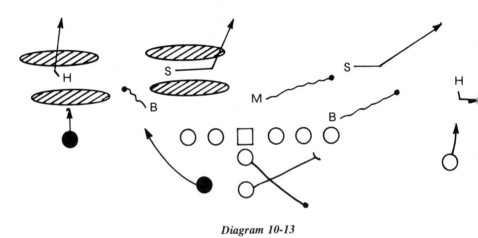

Diagram 10-13

The offense should attack the short areas immediately. With two receivers releasing to the throwback side, there are a multiple of routes that can be used. A big factor for the quarterback and receivers' success of the pass is the keying of the one available linebacker. Wherever he reacts, the quarterback should pass the ball opposite his movement. Two examples of this are indicated (Diagrams 10-14 and 10-15). In the first diagram, the split end executes a curl and the halfback releases to the flat. If the outside linebacker sprints to the curl area, the quarterback passes to the halfback in the flat or as he is turning upfield. If the defender sprints to the flat, the quarterback locates the curl receiver. The second diagram illustrates two square-out routes with simi-

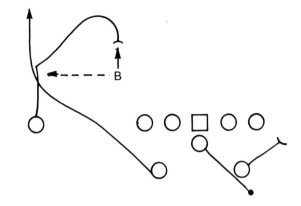

Diagram 10-14

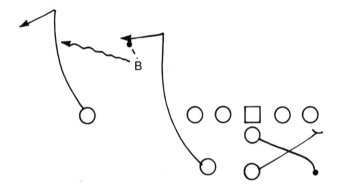

Diagram 10-15

lar principles applied. It is the quarterback's responsibility to deliver the ball to the receiver who is free.

Of course, many other patterns can evolve both short and long in attacking the four deep secondary coverages. The throwback pass should not be utilized until the defense is overreacting to the sprint or roll-out pass. Once this is shown, however, weakness areas toward the throwback side can easily be exploited. Other coverages may be seen, such as man-to-man or some man-zone combination. When this occurs, the offense should adopt routes that will successfully take advantage of these coverages.

11

Coaching the Quick Passing Game
for a High-Scoring Offense

The purpose of the quick passing game is to gain good, fast yardage, before the defense has the opportunity to react. The quarterback takes the snap from the center and passes immediately to a tight or wide receiver releasing from the line. This attack hopes to surprise the defense so it cannot cover the pass. The ball should be in the air or to the receiver before the defenders start to converge on the ball.

The quick passing game can pose a threat with any high-scoring offensive attack. The quick passing game can be utilized by the dropback, sprint-out, roll-out and play action series. In all cases, a good deal of planning and strategy should be developed in advance when attacking the defensive variations from game to game. Since the quick passing game routes are short, linebacker coverage becomes a factor. Linebacker alignments, and reaction before and after the snap of the ball, do become important factors for this pass to find success.

RECEIVER ROUTES FOR THE QUICK PASSING GAME

The wide-out routes usually executed are the hitch, quick-out, slant and in. Diagram 11-1 clearly illustrates these routes by a flanker.

The Hitch

The hitch is a 5 yard hook. The receiver releases from the line and drives the defender covering him straight back. On the fourth or fifth step, he plants the outside foot to halt any momentum forward. The receiver immediately

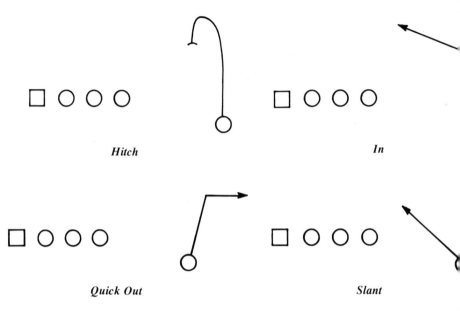

Diagram 11-1

pivots back toward the quarterback. At this time, the ball should be in the air. As he turns, the receiver should be aware that the ball will be delivered directly, and he must react to it wherever it is thrown. Once the receiver has caught the ball, he should be prepared for a quick hit by a defender. It is essential he tuck the ball under his arm tightly and try to turn upfield to get as much yardage as possible.

The Quick-Out

The quick-out is executed in the same manner as the hitch. However, on the fourth or fifth step, the receiver plants his inside foot so he can push off and turn to the outside. As he pivots, all the momentum is geared outside or back toward the line of scrimmage. His head and shoulders immediately snap around so he is looking toward the quarterback. The shoulders remain parallel to the line of scrimmage so he has the capability to catch a ball thrown inside or outside of him. Once the receiver initiates his break, he should be aware of the football immediately. Once the ball has been secured in his arms, he automatically pivots upfield for extra yardage.

The In Route

The receiver releases from the line as he did with the hitch and quick-out. However, on the fourth or fifth step the receiver plants his outside foot and breaks "in." He is running a crossing pattern across the field. It is not a 90 degree cut, as designed with the quick-out. Nor should the receiver run toward the post. It is a crossing maneuver attempting to break in front or behind linebackers. If the receiver has not caught the ball after the cut, he then tries to locate the open areas while he is on the move. The quarterback reads the same defensive reactions and passes the ball when the receiver is open.

The Slant

The slant is executed in a slightly different manner than was experienced with the other three. On the snap of the ball, the receiver releases from the line at a 45 degree angle and slants in toward the middle of the field. As the first couple of steps are initiated, the receiver glances into the quarterback. The quarterback is instructed to pass the ball as soon as the receiver is open. The slant pass is usually thrown immediately before the receiver runs into linebackers pursuing out from the formation. There are instances, however, when the ball is thrown after the receiver has gone beyond one or two linebackers. He therefore becomes open in the hook and middle areas of the passing lanes.

THE QUICK DROPBACK PASSING GAME

The quick dropback passing game is illustrated in Diagram 11-2 from a Pro-type formation. In each instance, both wide receivers execute the same

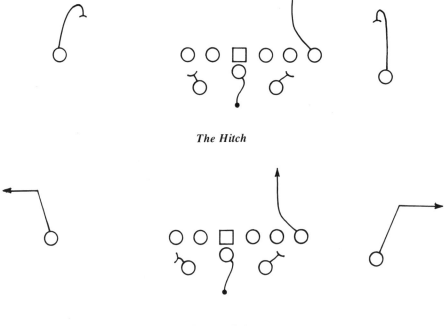

The Hitch

The Quick Out

Diagram 11-2

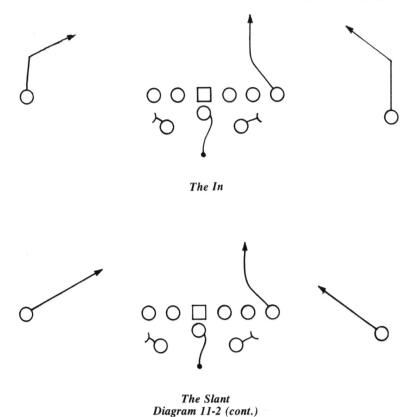

The In

The Slant
Diagram 11-2 (cont.)

route. The tight end slants in toward the middle as a safety valve. From a balanced stance, the quarterback initiates a three step drop. If he is a right handed passer, his first step is with the right foot. The second step is with the left, and the third and final foot placement is with the right. As the right foot is set, he should be prepared to throw right or left, depending upon what is open (Diagram 11-3). That decision can be established either prior to or after the snap of the ball. The ball should be brought to a good throwing position, as has been described previously.

Strategy of Attack

When the quick dropback passing series and routes are called, both wide receivers should run the same route. The tight end or inside halfback releases as an extra receiver. Some teams adopt the "hot receiver" principle with the inside man. On the snap of the ball, if the linebacker nearest the tight end stunts for the quarterback, the end yells, "Hot-Hot," and the quarterback throws the ball over the linebackers and to the receiver. However, the hot

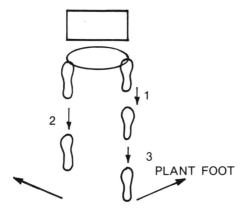

Diagram 11-3

receiver principle commands a considerable amount of time, drilling, and teaching. The offense must be fully committed to it if any success is to be established with this passing attack (Diagram 11-4).

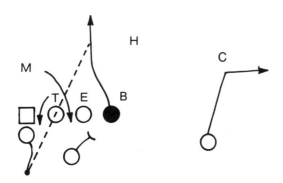

Diagram 11-4
The "Hot" Receiver

The quarterback reads the defensive alignment before the snap of the ball and decides which receiver is favorably open. There are many examples that can be illustrated. Defensive halfbacks can be aligned 8 to 10 yards off the line of scrimmage. Linebackers can be stationed near the placement of the ball and not be in a good alignment to quickly cover outside. The defensive coverage may be such that it cannot cover one or both receivers adequately. In any case, the decision to pass is determined before the snap. Once the quarterback knows who should get the ball, he simply sets on the third step

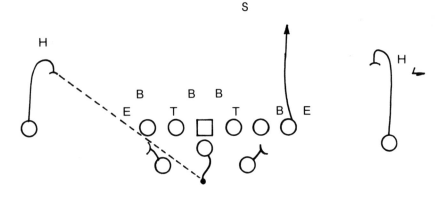

Diagram 11-5

The quarterback scans over the defensive alignment. On the left side, the outside linebacker is positioned inside the defensive end. The defensive halfback on the right is aligning tight on the flanker. The quarterback, therefore, turns to his left and passes to the split end.

and passes it to his open receiver. Diagram 11-5 illustrates an example of reading coverages before the ball is put into play.

Reading After the Snap of the Football

Reading after the ball is snapped must be achieved with precision and quick reaction. The quarterback has only a couple of seconds to decide whether to pass left or right. The decision is finalized by reading the weak safety. It is the safety (from a four spoke) who is positioned on the weak side of the formation. A three deep safety is considered the weak safety of an eight man front. The four spoke read is indicated in Diagram 11-6, and the three deep is shown in Diagram 11-7. If the weak safety remains in his position, runs backward, comes forward, or goes in any weak-side direction, the quarterback scans to the strong side. If, however, the weak safety begins to react toward the strength of the formation, the quarterback immediately throws to the weak side. Again, a great deal of time, effort, and teaching must be directed at the quarterback to have the passing game reading successful.

LINE BLOCKING

There are two methods the offensive line can use to block the quick dropback passing game. First, the blockers can be aggressive and cross the line of scrimmage as if it were a play action pass or running play. This serves two purposes. It prevents the defense from penetrating into the offensive backfield, and secondly, it forces the defenders to keep their hands down. They are trying to ward off the blockers. Since the pass is off in a matter of

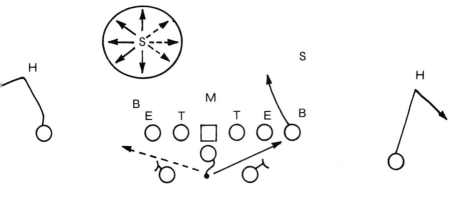

Diagram 11-6
The Quick-Out Pattern

*The quarterback throws strong (flanker) if the safety reacts weak;
and throws weak (split end), if the safety goes strong.*

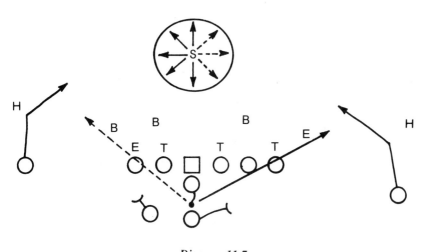

Diagram 11-7

seconds, the rushers and/or linebackers do not have the opportunity to knock
the pass down.

A second way to block for the quick pass is a form of cup protection.
Each blocker sets up as if it were a dropback pass, but shuffling back does not
occur. The blocker sets himself on the line of scrimmage and fights off the
defenders from that position. Whatever the techniques employed by the offensive unit, the rules mentioned previously for the dropback pass apply.

THE SPRINT-OUT QUICK PASS ATTACK

The quick passing game can easily be applied to the sprint-out pass. The sprint-out technique of the quarterback is advantageous because he is stepping or facing out from the offensive center, and can immediately see the receiver he is going to pass the ball to. The roll-out is quite different because the quarterback must reverse pivot. While the quick pass can be achieved from this action, it is not thrown as quickly. Also, the quarterback cannot see the open receiver immediately. Therefore, it is recommended the quarterback employ the sprint-out technique.

The quarterback technique of the step-out and the sprint is similar to the sprint-out pass. However, the quarterback must be ready to throw the ball on the second step coming away from the center. This is required because the quarterback should pass on the third step.

Strategy of Attack

The common routes for the receivers include the hitch, quick-out, slant, and in. Both sides of the formation (if two wide-outs are set) execute the same pattern, which was described in the dropback section. If only one wide-out is positioned, then the quarterback sprints to that particular side.

Unlike the dropback quick pass, the sprint-out attack cannot read the movements of the defense after the snap of the ball and then pass to either side of the formation. The quarterback does, however, have the opportunity to read defensive coverage before the snap and decide in which direction he is going to sprint. Once that decision is made, it cannot be changed. The receiver should have the opportunity (if only one wide-out is aligned) to alter the route stated in the huddle, if the defensive coverage is such that the route will not work. One clear example is with the slant pass. A slant is called, but a linebacker or defensive halfback aligns on the inside shoulder of the receiver. The receiver cannot release easily inside. Therefore, a method should be devised (a check on the line of scrimmage, a signal from the receiver to the quarterback, or just reading the alignment, etc.) for the receiver to alter his pattern. For example, a quick-in route could be substituted for the slant. Another example is indicated in Diagram 11-8. As can be seen, the split end is completely covered by the outside linebacker. An out route is called in the huddle, but it may not be successful. The split end, therefore, adjusts his route to a quick out and up. The quarterback sprints in the direction, waits for the receiver to turn upfield, and passes immediately to the open seam. The result is the linebacker turns away from the passer, and he does not have the opportunity to glance inside to notice if the ball is thrown.

Line Blocking

Line blocking, including rules and techniques, is exactly the same as the sprint-out pass. The only difference is that the line must be aware that the play is quick. The blocks do not have to be sustained long, and the linemen can release from their responsibility and cover the pass as soon as possible.

Two examples of the quick sprint-out passing game are illustrated in Diagrams 11-9 and 11-10. The first example indicates one wide-out covered

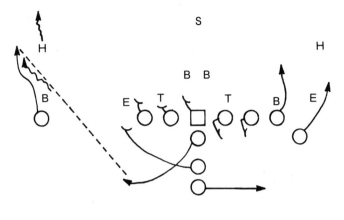

Diagram 11-8

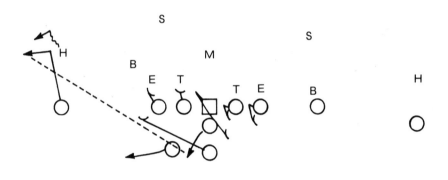

Diagram 11-9

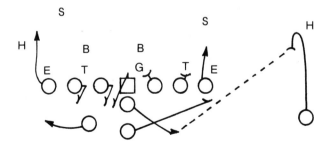

Diagram 11-10

by a tight defensive halfback and, therefore, the quarterback sprints in the opposite direction. The second illustration shows one wide-out formation with the receiver executing the hitch pattern.

False Keys

Utilzing false keys against the defensive coverage will make the quick passing game more effective. One example is illustrated in Diagram 11-11. Many teams use zone coverage and key the fullback for rotation. When this is known, the offense can send the fullback one way, forcing rotation toward him, and sprint the quarterback in the opposite direction. This offers the receiver a better opportunity to catch the ball. Also, it forces a one on one situation, in which the receiver can outmaneuver the defensive halfback before and after the ball is caught.

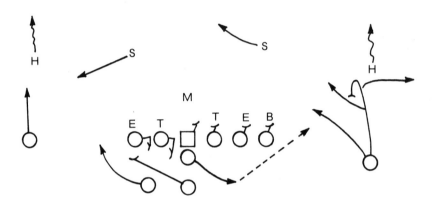

Diagram 11-11

QUICK PASSING FROM PLAY ACTION PASSES

Play action utilizes quick passes, but in a different manner. A running play is faked into the line and the pass is delivered immediately. The quick pass is usually combined with a quick hitting play into the line. Usually, the more common routes utilized from both the dropback and sprint-out attacks are not employed. However, one or two could be adopted. The purpose of the quick hitting play action pass is to freeze linebackers in their positions so they have difficulty getting into their respective coverage areas. It is used to attack quick linebackers or linebackers who pursue very well. The linebackers vacate an area, with the receiver exploiting the weakness. Another aspect is the element of surprise. Quick and substantial yardage can be gained on a quick pass to a receiver just over the line of scrimmage. In most cases he is open, and a one on one situation with a defensive halfback occurs.

As previously mentioned, the quick pass should be used with a rapidly hitting play. A simplified pass is indicated in Diagram 11-12. The wishbone fullback drives into the line to hold the Oklahoma 5-4 linebacker. The tight end releases directly upfield, and the quarterback passes the ball after the fake is initiated to the fullback. An excellent pass accompanying this play is to fake the fullback veer, and then fake the quick pass to the tight end (Diagram 11-13). The quarterback drops straight back and passes to the wingback swinging downfield. In most cases, the wingback pass is successful after the quick pass is completed to the tight end. The defensive halfback and corner-back usually react quickly to stop it. When this occurs, the quarterback sets and delivers the ball to the wingback.

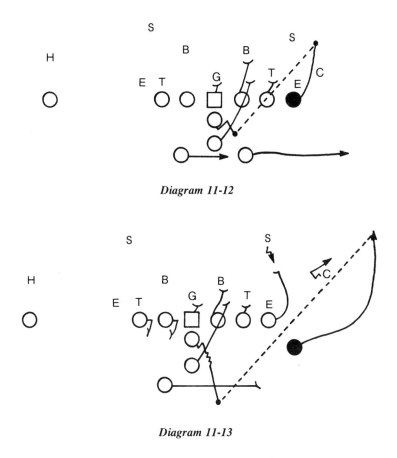

Diagram 11-12

Diagram 11-13

An example of strategically attacking quick pursuing linebackers is illustrated in Diagram 11-14. The straight ahead dive is used. The linebacker on the left overly pursues the "dive" back. The quarterback steps back and passes to the tight end releasing into the vacated area.

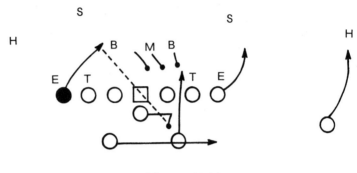

Diagram 11-14

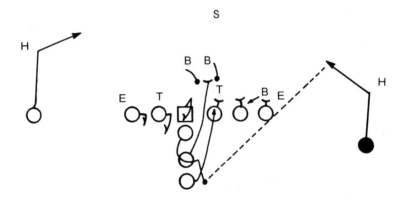

Diagram 11-15

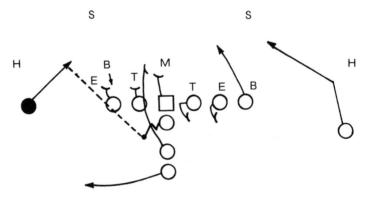

Diagram 11-16

Wide-out receivers can also be used with the quick hitting pass. Two examples are indicated in Diagrams 11-15 and 11-16. In Diagram 11-15, the quarterback fakes the isolation series to the "I" tailback. The quarterback reverse pivots, initiates a quick fake to the halfback, sets up, and delivers the ball to the flanker, executing an "in" route. The ball is thrown whenever the receiver is open. In Diagram 11-16, a slant pattern is used by the split end with a fake to the fullback over the left guard. Again, the pass is completed in the open passing lanes between linebackers.

Many other quick play action passes can be employed by the offensive team. Passes should be geared with the successful running plays in the offense. Intelligent and imaginative strategy should also be used.

12

Attacking Defenses with
the Play Action Pass

Play action passes are an instrumental
and essential part of any high-scoring passing offense. Any time the quarterback can fake a successful running action, and freeze defenders in their
positions, the easier it becomes to complete the pass. The play action pass is a
beneficial supplement to the other passing phases of the offense, i.e., sprint-
out, roll-out, dropback, etc. A quarterback who is not a particularly good
passer can utilize various play action techniques to better foster the passing
game.

THE ADVANTAGES OF THE PLAY ACTION PASS

The advantages of the play action pass are as follows:

1. The quarterback fakes into the line with a potential ball carrier,
   tending to hold both the defensive linemen and linebackers in their
   positions.
2. The defensive secondary can not cover its respective defensive
   areas as quickly because of the fake.
3. Certain receivers can release into defensive zones or pass lanes
   quickly (especially receivers from the offside). Usually, the defenders will not initially see them, or will not react to them quickly
   enough.
4. The quarterback can either set or roll-out in either direction, without the defense having knowledge of exactly where he will be
   located.

5. The defensive rush is greatly decelerated, because of where the fake is completed, and where the quarterback maneuvers.

6. Offensive backs can seep into the coverage unnoticed, because of the fake(s) into the line.

SEQUENCES AND PLAY ACTION PASSES

There are numerous series or sequences of plays in football today. The various sequences comprise the wishbone veer, split-veer, power, outside belly, inside belly, split-T, isolation, crossbucks, Delaware-T, etc. With the different plays used by each series, there can be various play action passes developed. When designing play action passes, it is best to have them evolve from the most used and successful running plays in the series. An example would be from the power series. If the off-tackle power run is the best running play in the power sequence, the coach should design a play action pass derived from the off-tackle play. If the fullback veer play from the wishbone series is the most successful, a play action pass should be developed off its action. Many other examples could be discussed, but these will suffice.

The number of play action passes should be taken into account. If one series is used by a team, a number of play action looks can be derived. If two series are utilized within the offensive system, then other play action passes must develop from these series. However, if a team is a multiple offense with many series, less play action passes should be run from each series, because practice and proficiency become factors.

QUARTERBACK TECHNIQUES WITH THE PLAY ACTION PASS

Whenever a play action pass is used, it is important the quarterback execute the pass as if it were the actual running play. Similar steps, body movement, and hand coordination with the faking back should be accomplished with precision. It must look as if the back is definitely receiving the football. Once the play is faked, most actions roll-out or set up in the designated area.

There are good coaching points that can be given to the quarterback. Eye and head movement is very significant. Once the quarterback has faked the offensive back into the line, he should begin moving to the appropriate position for the pass. However, as he does so, he continues to look at the faking back as if *he* has the football. If he can continue to glance at him for one or two seconds, it may help draw linebackers and/or other defenders to the faking back. This easily widens the passing lanes needed for the quarterback.

Shoulder, arm, and hand movement is also essential in some faking action. This is true with bootleg or waggle passes. As the quarterback delivers the fake, and watches the faking ball carrier go by, he can place his hand into the pocket of the offensive back. By accomplishing this, the quarterback is extending his hand and arm, and turning his shoulder toward the halfback. If the quarterback can extend this body movement for the next two or three steps, while the faking back continues, it may tend to hold or freeze pass defenders from their responsibilities. The football is held with the hand firmly against the stomach so a fumble or any jostling of the ball does not occur.

Another technique utilized in many play action passes is for the quarterback to hold the football on the back portion of the upper leg or near the thigh. This technique usually results on a running type fake into the line, with the quarterback sprinting outside the defensive end toward the same side as the faking offensive back. One example is the outside belly pass off the fake of the outside belly play. The quarterback reverse pivots and places the ball into the pocket of the fullback. As the fake is near its completion, the quarterback pushes off the inside foot, and steps away from the line of scrimmage and outside around the defensive end. As he does so, the football is taken out of the pocket and brought to the outside side portion of the upper leg, hidden from the defenders. The opposite hand flows with the faking back as if the ball was handed off. In reality, however, the quarterback is attaining depth and width on his roll with the ball, out of the defense's vision. After four or five steps are completed, the quarterback brings the ball up to the passing position, prepared to throw.

BACKFIELD TECHNIQUES WITH THE PLAY ACTION PASS

The offensive back faking the play action pass must be a good actor. His takeoff, steps, and body movement should all be geared to have the play look similar to a run. Similar techniques and fundamentals, including forming the pocket for the ball, keeping the head up, scanning for the hole, and running with reckless abandon are key elements for the success of the play action pass. Once the fake has been carried out, the back should continue to run with authority into and through the hole. If he is tackled by the defense, his fake should be considered a good one.

Other offensive backs may not be receivers, but are used for the play action as well. Since they are usually blockers or decoying backs, their initial movement and backfield course is the same also. If a back is used to block a defender (a defensive end), he should take a course similar to that of the running play. If the motion and backfield flow looks similar for both the run and the pass, the offense will have greater success with its play action passes.

RECEIVER TECHNIQUES WITH THE PLAY ACTION PASS

There are many offensive techniques a pass receiver can employ with play action passes. Many of them depend upon the split of the receiver. For example, if the receiver splits wide from the formation, he can release easily and drive downfield as if to execute a block. Different techniques can be used. He can utilize head and shoulder fakes, various acceleration or deceleration movements, and different paths of travel—all to have the play action look similar to the run.

If the receiver is tight, he has a number of movements he can perform. Many of them depend upon the timing of the fake in the backfield, width and depth of the formation, etc. In most cases, the receiver blocks his running responsibility for one or two counts, and then releases into the coverage on his route. He attempts to locate the open areas that develop after the fake of the play.

OFFENSIVE LINE TECHNIQUES WITH THE PLAY ACTION PASS

The most important coaching point for the line is that they must attack the defensive front nearest the faking back, as if it is a run. They should strike out and through the numbers of their respective assignments, so the defenders do not immediately realize it is a pass. The opposite side is different. The blocking rules will depend upon the type of play it is. However, the techniques do change. The line does not have to be as aggressive. In many cases, they can set back and wait for the defenders to rush. If it is a bootleg pass, though, the techniques alter. While it is not as passive or aggressive, the line blocks its assignments on the line of scrimmage and does not permit penetration. In every play action pass, however, common sense prevails. If the fake is in one direction, the line is aggressive. Depending where the quarterback goes, the line will block accordingly—whether it be very passive (setting up), or more aggressive (blocking on the line of scrimmage).

CATEGORIES OF PLAY ACTION PASSES

While there are numerous and different play action passes, every one can be categorized into one of five main areas.

1. The Roll-Out
2. The Semi-Roll
3. The Bootleg
4. The Waggle
5. The Dropback

The Roll-Out

This play action pass has the fake of the play and the pass going in the same direction. The passer fakes the offensive back into the line and continues on attempting to break containment outside the defensive end. All the routes are usually geared in the same direction toward the sideline.

The Semi-Roll

The semi-roll is similar to the roll-out, except after the fake is completed, the quarterback begins to roll outside. However, he pulls up approximately behind the original tight end's position. The pass routes can now be directed either outside or inside, depending upon what is being attacked.

The Bootleg

A bootleg is a fake of the backfield toward the strength of a formation while the passer drives outside in the opposite direction. Backfield flow hopes to force defenders opposite that of the actual play action designed. The pass routes are directed to the side of the quarterback roll and opposite that of the linebacker and secondary initial flow.

The Waggle

The waggle pass is similar to the bootleg. However, the flow of the backfield fake is toward the weak side of the formation. The passer rolls outside to the strength where, in most cases, two quick receivers are releasing from the line.

The Dropback

The drop of a quarterback from the line and setting in a pocket is another method. The fake of the backs can be either toward or away from the actual pass pattern. The quarterback sets up and can now scan the entire field or a specific side. Pass routes can also be geared in either direction.

ATTACKING WITH THE PLAY ACTION PASS

Attacking procedures with the play action pass are similar to the other pass actions. Some of the attacking considerations are:

1. Attack defensive alignments and weakness areas
2. Attack out of position defenders
3. Attack the defenders over and under *reactions*

Attack Defensive Alignments and Weaknesses

The alignment and the weakness areas of the defensive scheme should be attacked. The location of the defensive linebackers and their distance to their coverage areas must be exploited. Secondary capabilities and coverages should also be attacked.

Attack Out of Position Defenders

Defenders aligned out of position must be attacked. This may be due to the formation (width and depth) used. If a linebacker is nearer the offensive set, rather than the wide receiver, the offense can attack wide. Proper strategical attack is achieved as mentioned in previous attacking chapters.

Attack the Defenders Over and Under Reactions

The greatest advantage of the play action pass is its ability to create passing lanes and areas due to the reactions of the defenders. Since linebackers nearest the play fake must honor the faking back, passing areas open automatically. Since the linebackers cannot react quickly enough to their respective areas, the chances of a pass completion increase. However, linebackers away from the play fake have a tendency to overreact to the play fake, which can open other valuable passing space for the quarterback. Man-to-man coverages have been greatly exploited. There have been many instances when receivers become completely free because the linebacker or secondary defender reacted too quickly to the fake.

PLAY ACTION PASSES FROM VARIOUS SERIES

Every play action pass cannot be illustrated in this chapter. A book could be written on that subject alone. However, a sampling of various play action passes, with routes and blocking, are indicated for the five sequences of plays mentioned. These are successful play action passes that are utilized for a purpose. They are used as an element of surprise, to outwit the defense, to attack a certain defender or defenders, to attack a defensive weakness area, to outposition a defender, and/or to attack the reaction of the linebackers and secondary. Other play action possibilities are indicated in Chapter 10.

The Power Series

The most common passes dealt within the power series are the bootleg, waggle, and halfback passes. Diagram 12-1 illustrates the bootleg pass, while Diagram 12-2 shows the halfback throwing the football.

The Outside Belly Series

An excellent pass from the outside belly series is the roll-out by the quarterback. The fake is initiated inside, with offensive pressure being placed on the defensive end and halfback or corner area. Diagram 12-3 illustrates the outside belly pass.

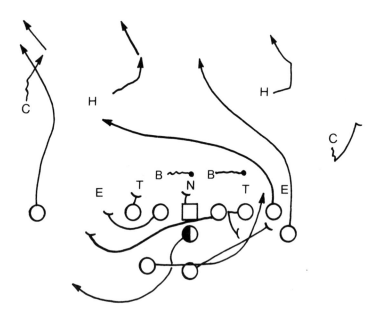

Diagram 12-1

The backfield flows to the right, faking the off-tackle power play. The quarterback reverses, but fakes to the halfback, and attempts to attain depth on the roll-out. The offensive line nearest the boot action attacks the defenders on the line of scrimmage. The offside guard pulls for depth and tries to hook the defensive end in. If the defensive end gains depth upfield, the guard knocks him outside. The split end executes a flag route. The tight end drags across field, looking for any open areas away from the linebackers. The wingback attempts to drive the defensive secondary deep. The split end can be given other routes best suited for the defensive scheme. These include the square-out, comeback, curl, post, etc.

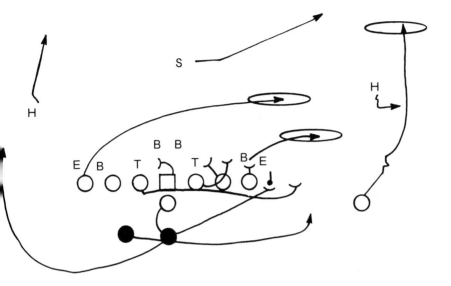

Diagram 12-2

The quarterback hands the ball off to the offensive left halfback.
The frontside line and fullback block aggressively, so the play
looks similar to a sweep. The guard pulls as in the run, but slows
to protect the passer. The flanker releases as if to block the defensive halfback and then sprints to the flag. The tight end blocks for
two counts and releases for the open areas in the flat. The backside
end crosses and drives for the curl area, 15 to 18 yards deep. The
quarterback, after handing the ball off, continues outside. He
reads the secondary coverage, but continues on as a receiver. The
passing halfback has the opportunity to either throw the "bomb"
to the flanker or direct his pass to the shorter routes. If the quarterback finds himself open on the other side of the field, he should
alert the halfback the next time it is thrown.

The Tailback to Daylight Series

With the tailback running off-tackle from the "I" position, it provides
him the opportunity to cut back along the line of scrimmage for any open
running area. It also provides an excellent method for a complete passing
attack. The tailback fakes at the off-tackle position, with the fullback blocking
the defensive end. The entire line blocks solid along the line. Once the fake
has been initiated, the quarterback can drop back into a pocket position and
have an entire view of the defensive coverage. Patterns can be executed to
both the front or backside. Diagrams 12-4 through 12-6 illustrate three examples of this play action, with patterns designed from it.

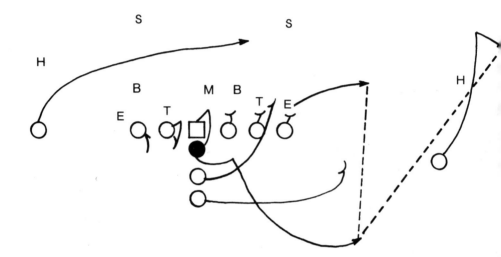

Diagram 12-3

*The fullback is the faking back. He drives through the outside hip
of the offensive tackle, hoping to hold or freeze the defensive end.
The tailback runs parallel to the line of scrimmage and maneuvers
upfield for the defensive end. The quarterback reverse pivots and
delivers a good fake into the line. Once the fake is completed, he
pulls the ball from the fullback's pocket, places it on the outside
portion of his leg, and attempts to drive outside for the corner
area. Any pattern can be executed. In this case, the flanker does a
square-out, while the tight end blocks and drives for the open area
in the flat. The offside end drags. The onside linemen aggressively
block their assignments.*

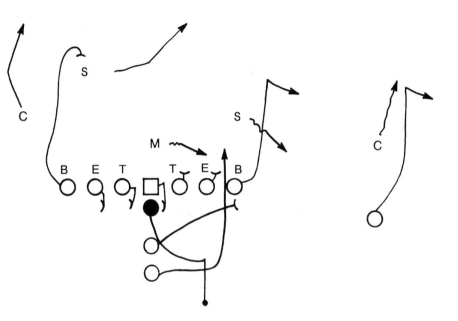

Diagram 12-4

As indicated, the fullback blocks out on the first man located outside the offensive tackle's block. The onside of the line is aggressive, showing run action. The backside, however, sets for pocket protection. The quarterback reverse pivots and initiates a good fake with the tailback. The tailback continues on through the line. If a coach finds the tailback is not being tackled, he can be used as a pass receiver. The flanker and tight end execute deep square-out routes. This is done because the fake takes time to develop before the quarterback sets up. Since it is a delayed play, the routes can be longer. The backside end runs a hook route.

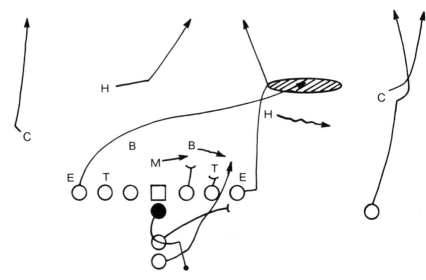

Diagram 12-5

Similar blocking and backfield fakes occur. The flanker and tight end execute post routes in order to drive the defensive secondary deep. The quarterback sets and looks for the drag route coming across the field underneath these deep routes.

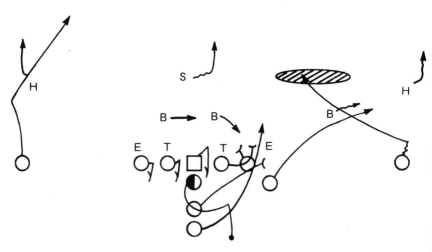

Diagram 12-6

A pick pattern is illustrated. The slot back drives to the flat hoping to occupy the outside linebacker. The wide receiver releases from the line slowly, but drives underneath the slot back's route. If he does not receive the ball immediately, he maneuvers upfield away from the inside linebackers. The inside linebackers, however, should be held by the fake.

The Split Veer Series

With the triple option exploiting defenses today as never before, offenses are utilizing the split back offense, and adding two receivers wide, whether they are on the same or opposite sides. Diagrams 12-7 and 12-8 illustrate two successful patterns against defensive schemes trying to halt both the triple option and the passing game.

Isolation Series

While many routes and patterns can be developed from this series, a bootleg pass is indicated in Diagram 12-9.

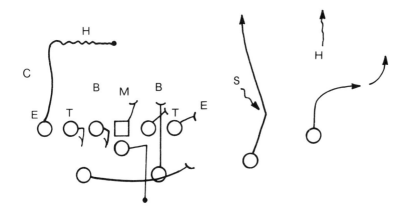

Diagram 12-7

The quarterback and inside wide receiver read the secondary coverage before and after the snap of the ball. The wide slot back drives upfield for five steps and breaks to the inside. Whether it be invert or rotational coverage, the receiver angles upfield away from the weak-side defensive safety. If man-to-man coverage is used, the slot back attempts to outrace the safety for the goal line. The quarterback initiates a quick fake to the halfback and sets back. He tries to throw the ball instantly when the receiver is open. This is usually when he makes his break. The wide split end executes a quick-out. If the ball is not delivered, he immediately turns up the side line. The backside end runs a hook route. Blocking is slightly altered. The guard's responsibility is the number 1 lineman, while the tackle's is the number 2 man. The diving halfback blocks the first linebacker, while the offside halfback is employed for added protection.

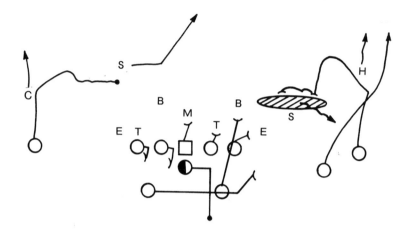

Diagram 12-8

The line blocking and backfield execution remain the same. A common route is accomplished by the two wide receivers. A curl route is run by the wide receiver, while the inside wide-out executes an up route. The curl should be well open, since the outside linebacker is held in with the diving halfback.

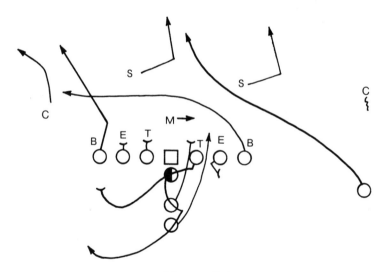

Diagram 12-9

The tailback drives over the guard area, as he does with the isolation play. The quarterback reverse pivots, initiates a good fake, and begins to roll outside in a bootleg fashion. The onside line blocks on the line of scrimmage, while the offside guard pulls to block the defensive end. The fullback blocks over the guard area. The left end drives for the flag, while the offside end drags across field. The flanker attempts to go deep.

13

Utilizing Screens and Draws
with a High-Scoring
Passing Offense

Draws and screens are an essential aspect to any successful passing attack. They can be used to outwit, surprise or outmaneuver the defense. They are considered the counters or reverses of the passing game. When pass completions are minimized due to any reason, it is usually the draw or screen that can gain the necessary yardage.

DRAWS

The draw employed is dependent upon the passing action of the offense. If a team is consistently utilizing the dropback pass, the draw should be executed from that series. The same is true with the sprint-out also. The sprint-out draw is an excellent play. It can gain good yardage by putting pressure on the outside linebackers and defensive end. As can be seen, therefore, there are two categories of draws, i.e., the dropback, and the sprint-out.

WHEN TO USE THE DRAW

When to use the draw as a counter threat is an important factor. The following are points to consider. The draw can be used:

1. As an element of surprise. An offense can utilize it whether the passing game has had success or not.
2. To attack different alignments. Some defensive teams place their

linebackers deeper than usual in passing situations. When this is spotted, the draw should be run.

3.   If linebackers are achieving depth quickly to stop the underneath pass.

4.   When defensive pass rushers consistently lose their proper rush lane and continue to drive either inside or outside, creating holes for the draw.

5.   When the penetrating defenders are placing quick pressure on the quarterback so he does not have ample time to pass.

THE DROPBACK DRAW

The passing percentage of an offense should be the factor to determine the style and amount of draws executed within the offense. If the dropback pass is used 10 to 20 per cent of the time, possibly only one draw should be used. However, if the dropback plays a large part (40 to 60 per cent) of the offensive attack, two or three different draws may be used.

The draw can be run by either the halfback, fullback or both. It can be executed from a pro set, a normal set, or from the "I" formation. The ball can be handed off in front of the ball carrier or behind him.

THE FRONT HAND-OFF DRAW

The front hand-off draw is illustrated in Diagram 13-1. The quarterback drop steps away from the center, exactly as he does in dropback pass situation. He can utilize either the cross-over or back pedal technique. If he is a right handed passer, and handing off to the right, it is a matter of just slipping the ball into the pocket of the ball carrier. This is attained with the opposite hand on approximately the third step (cross-over technique). The quarterback continues to drop back trying to force rushers deeper and wider and momentarily holding the linebackers and secondary.

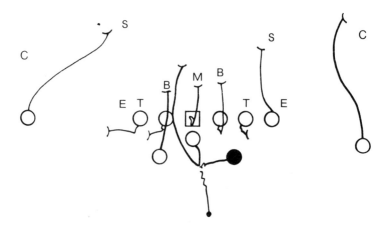

Diagram 13-1

Wherever the ball carrier is aligned in the backfield, he must adjust to a position between the center and offensive guard to receive the hand-off. While the ball carrier is waiting for the football, he acts as if he is an added blocker for the passer. The opposite back also fakes for a count. His assignment is the linebacker to the side of the play. If the linebacker stunts, he attacks him immediately, and attempts to knock him down by going through his knees. However, if the linebacker starts to his respective pass coverage, the back attacks him wherever he goes.

LINE RULES AND TECHNIQUES

The line rules are rather easy to learn and are as follows:

1. Center—Block on, linebacker on or offside

2. Onside Guard—Block the 1st defender on the line of scrimmage

3. Onside Tackle—Block the 2nd defender on the line of scrimmage

4. Offside Guard—Block the 1st defender on the line of scrimmage (Odd Defense—Block LB)

5. Offside Tackle—Block the 2nd defender on the line of scrimmage (Odd Defense—Block the 1st defender)

6. Ends and other Receivers—Release from the line and block downfield in front of the play

The offensive line techniques for the dropback draw are consistent with the dropback pass. The line sets back quickly, as if it is actually a pass. They remain low and show all the techniques necessary for good pass protection. However, after approximately one count, the blockers attack their respective defenders. They "ride" the rushers in the direction of their travel, and let the back cut off the blocks.

If the draw is directed to the opposite side of center, the quarterback's hand-off technique changes slightly. After the third cross-over step is completed, he pivots 180 degrees off that step. He dips slightly at the hips for the turn, and gives the football to the ball carrier with his right hand. Once the back secures the hand-off, the quarterback continues the drop, hoping to delay any defenders from the ball (Diagram 13-2).

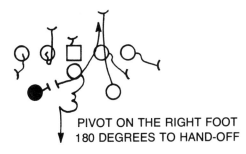

PIVOT ON THE RIGHT FOOT
180 DEGREES TO HAND-OFF

Diagram 13-2

THE BACK HAND-OFF DRAW

The back hand-off draw is illustrated in Diagram 13-3. The purpose of the draw is to force pass rushers deeper, and to hold the linebackers and secondary longer. It is a deceiving draw because the quarterback drops past the ball carrier. When this is executed, the defense reacts even more to the pass look. However, once the quarterback goes beyond the halfback, he slows down and slips the ball into his pocket. The ball carrier holds for a longer count, waits for the quarterback to go past him, and slides into the original path of the quarterback. With the quarterback's deceleration, the halfback turns his shoulders perpendicular to the line and forms a pocket for the quarterback. The ball is slipped in and the halfback scans for the open running areas. Blocking and other techniques for the line and backs remain the same.

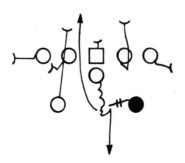

Diagram 13-3

THE HOT RECEIVER DRAW

The hot receiver principle can be effective with the dropback draw. Since the draw is not a particularly good play versus the stunting game, the hot receiver concept is an added device for offensive success. Diagram 13-4

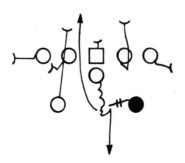

Diagram 13-4

indicates the tight end as the hot receiver. He releases from the line and reads the linebacker to his side. If he does not stunt, the end continues upfield to block. If, however, the linebacker blitzes forward, the end yells "hot-hot," and looks for the football. Also, the quarterback drops and keys the linebacker. If he stunts forward, the quarterback lofts the ball over his head to the end. If he does not, however, the quarterback merely hands the ball to the back. Blocking and all other responsibilities remain similar.

THE DRAW SWEEP

Another draw method derived from the dropback is the draw sweep. It can be blocked and executed a number of ways. Diagram 13-5 illustrates one method. The backfield remains similar to that in the other draws. However, the offensive line employs blocking combinations so the backside guard can pull and lead the ball carrier. The frontside line is aggressive, and blocking is similar to a power play. The timing between the blocking back and the offside guard is good because of the back's delay. This becomes a good draw because of the defensive end's penetration toward the quarterback's drop action, and also because of the linebacker's backward movement.

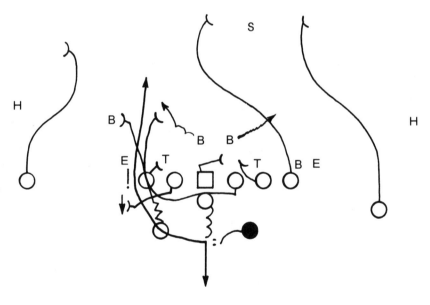

Diagram 13-5

THE SPRINT-OUT DRAW

The sprint-out draw (Diagram 13-6) is a popular feature in today's offensive attack. It creates a great deal of pressure on the defensive ends and corner areas. Since the play starts out in the same fashion as the sprint-out, and

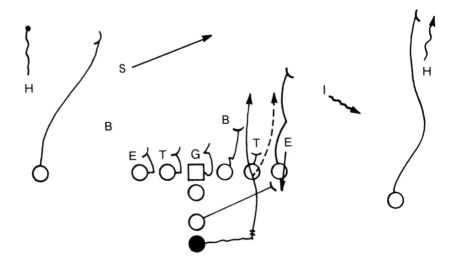

Diagram 13-6

because it is delayed, the defensive end is not sure whether to widen, penetrate, or close down in order to halt the draw or sprint-out pass. Linebackers are put into a bind also. They are not sure whether to drop into their coverage, decelerate and look for the draw, or completely wait until the hand-off point is reached to know who has the ball.

QUARTERBACK TECHNIQUES

The quarterback's action is similar to the face-out or open-step of the sprint-out pass. After taking the snap from center, the quarterback aims at a forty-five degree angle away from the line of scrimmage to a point behind the offensive tackle. He should reach this spot by the fifth step. The quarterback initiates a front hand-off to the tailback, who is at the same position. After the ball is inserted, the quarterback continues outside as if he has the ball. This may help widen the end and momentarily hold other linebacker and secondary defenders.

TAILBACK TECHNIQUES

The sprint-out draw is best run from an "I" tailback set. On the snap of the ball, the tailback open steps parallel to the line of scrimmage. On this third step he plants and aims over the offensive tackle's alignment. As he pivots, he should have his arm and hands in position for the hand-off. Once he receives the football, he cuts and drives off the block of the tackle. The block of the tackle is dependent upon the defense and its subsequent movement. In most cases, if the defense does not stunt, the defensive tackle maneuvers outside in pursuit of the sprint look. If this occurs, the tailback cuts inside of him. However, if the defensive tackle stunts inside, the tailback naturally runs outside.

The blocking described is dependent upon the release of the offensive tight end or whether the end is split or not. A few teams desire a double team on the defensive tackle and, therefore, a tight end is necessary. If this is the case, the tailback's route will differ slightly. His aiming point is the outside leg of the offensive tackle. In most instances, the tailback will run outside the double team block.

FULLBACK'S TECHNIQUES

The fullback begins similar action to that of the regular sprint-out. He attacks the defensive end in the same fashion. By doing so, the defensive end does not know whether it is a run or pass. If there is a slight variation to the fullback's course, the defensive end can spot it and know whether to halt the draw or pass. Once the fullback reaches the defensive end, he drives his head through the end's crotch to knock him down.

OFFENSIVE LINE

The offensive line rules remain the same as for the sprint-out. However, the techniques change. The frontside line aggressively attacks the defenders and stays with them. If a linebacker is positioned over any one of them, they should pause for a count (to show pass) and then attack. The backside shows pass for one second also, and attacks its assignments. The receivers release from the line, as if it is a pass, and try to maneuver in front of the ball carrier.

SCREENS

There are many and various styles of screen passes. Screens are executed from every series in football. They are thrown to almost every conceivable position and from every formation. Tight ends, split ends, flankers, slot backs, halfbacks, and fullbacks all receive screen passes.

When Screens Are Used

Screen passes can be employed any time on almost any area of the field. The following are some of the points to consider.

1. A screen can be used as an element of surprise.
2. Screens can be utilized to beat alignments of width and depth.
3. A screen is useful when defenses are creating a great deal of pressure, either through the normal rush or by blitzing.

BEING GOOD ACTORS

Every player on the offensive team must be an actor. Whatever the screen comes off of, i.e., dropback, sprint, play action, etc., the quarterback, faking backfield, and line must perform their assignments so the screen looks similar to the original play. For example, if the screen is executed from dropback action, the quarterback must set up, scan downfield, and look as if he is going to pass. At the last moment, however, he scrambles backwards, looking as if he is in trouble. At that point, he lofts the ball to the screen runner. The offensive line must perform in the same careful manner. They set up, force the defenders on their rushing lanes, and slip into the screen behind them. The release of the line is important. If the linemen release in front of the eyes of the defenders, the rushers can spot the screen. If, however, the release is behind, the better the opportunity the screen has for success.

CATEGORIES OF SCREENS

Screen passes can be placed into three categories. Each category, however, can have different formations and receivers. Following are the categories and subdivisions of screen passes.

A. Dropback
1. Ball Carrier to Formation's Strength
2. Ball Carrier to Formation's Weak Side
3. Ball Carrier to the Flood Side
4. A Double Screen to Both Sides
5. A Delay Double Screen
6. A Quick Screen
7. A Middle Screen

B. Sprint (Roll)-Out
1. Ball Carrier to Sprint Side
2. Ball Carrier away from Sprint Side
3. Sprint Flood Screen

C. Play Action Screen
1. Quick Play Action
2. Delayed Play Action

SCREEN RULES

Screens can be executed easily, as long as the rules are plain and simple. For example, if a screen develops from dropback, the rules governing that particular action or series should remain the same for everyone, with only the designated linemen and back slipping into the screen. When flooding a zone with three receivers to one side, the flood rules are used. Screen rules, however, are maintained with certain linemen and the remaining back entering into it. Again, the other players block according to their flood rules and responsibilities. As can be seen, screen techniques incorporated within pass blocking series are easy. A multiple passing offense can add various screens to its repertoire without losing any of its proficiency.

EXAMPLE OF SCREENS

As mentioned previously, there are many and varied forms of screens from every action in football. Following are successful screens that have been employed at one time or another. The different categories are indicated. While only certain receivers are shown, other receivers can be utilized with similar blocking and backfield actions.

Dropback Screens

1. Ball Carrier to Strength of Formation (Diagram 13-7)

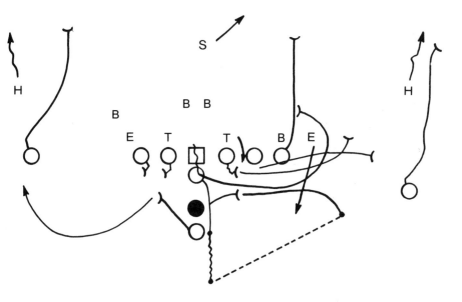

Diagram 13-7

This is a simplified screen to the formation's strength (flanker). The flanker, tight end, and split end release and block their respective 1/3 of the field. The quarterback drops away from the line of scrimmage and sets at his normal depth. When the defensive pressure is near, he automatically drops further, as if in trouble. The tailback utilizes his flare control rules, and blocks or releases according to the defensive movement. The fullback does the same. However, once the defensive rushers have penetrated past him, he quickly slides approximately three yards outside the original tight end's position. He turns outside (over his right shoulder) for the football. The offensive line employs dropback blocking rules. The offside guard and tackle continue to block as if it is a normal pass. The onside tackle, guard, and center block for two counts, release behind the defensive rush and sprint to their respective areas. The tackle's responsibility is to block any defender coming from the outside in. The guard protects the middle while the center scans inside for any pursuers. When the ball is caught, the ball carrier yells "go" and the blockers move upfield to block.

2. Ball Carrier to Weak Side of Formation (Diagram 13-8)

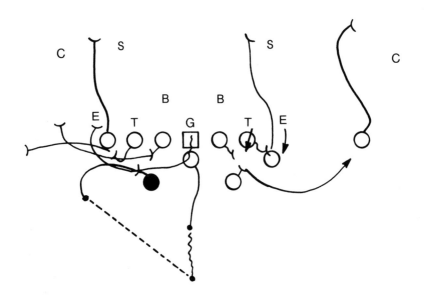

Diagram 13-8

*A similar screen is indicated away from the strength of the forma-
tion. All the receivers release to show pass, and then block their
assignments. The onside tackle, guard and center employ similar
responsibilities. The left halfback blocks for two counts and slips
into the screen area.*

3. Ball Carrier to the Flood Side (Diagram 13-9)

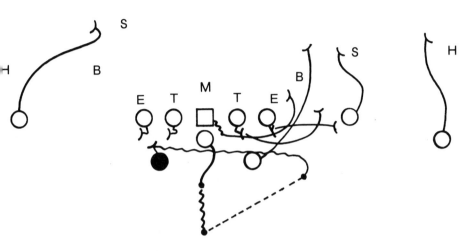

Diagram 13-9

A three man release is demonstrated to the strength of the formation. The receivers flood the area, but block their responsibilities. The quarterback drops to his normal depth, and only goes further backwards when the pressure gains on him. The line utilizes flood blocking assignments, with the frontside tackle, guard, and center still maneuvering to the screen area. In this case, the remaining halfback (left) blocks for two counts and quickly slides behind the rush to the screen area. While not illustrated, a flood screen can be executed to the weak side. The split end and left halfback flood the weak zones, with the right halfback moving in to the left screen.

4. A Double Screen (Diagram 13-10)

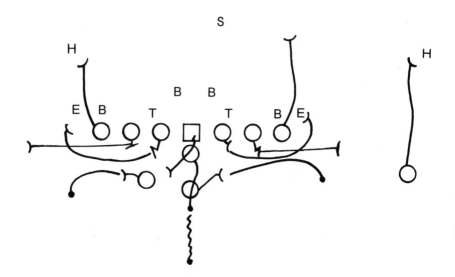

Diagram 13-10

The double screen illustrates both tackles and guards releasing to either side. Both backs block for two counts, and then do the same. The quarterback has the choice to throw to either side. The purpose of this screen is to have one back open if the other one is covered. The center remains in to block, while all receivers release and block their assignments.

5. A Delay (Double) Screen (Diagram 13-11)

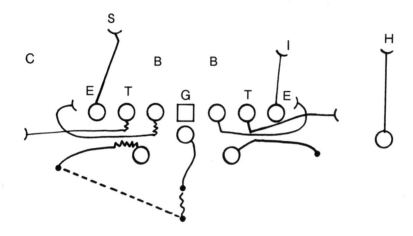

Diagram 13-11

As illustrated, the right tackle, guard, and right halfback block for one count and go to the screen area. They are decoys trying to show the defense a screen to the right. However, the actual screen is left. The left guard, tackle, and halfback block for as long as possible (two or three counts) before releasing to the screen. The quarterback drops back and looks to the decoying right halfback in the fake screen. Once the defense reacts in this direction, he immediately turns left and throws to the delaying left halfback.

6. The Quick Screen (Diagram 13-12)

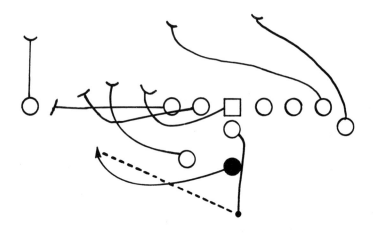

Diagram 13-12

The quick screen is different because there is absolutely no delay for the line or backs. At the snap of the ball, the quarterback drops back, turns, and immediately flips the ball to the back (fullback). The tackle, guard, and center release immediately to the screen area. The split end and left halfback release to block. The fullback sprints outside (in this case, left), gains some depth in the back-field, and looks over the inside shoulder for the ball.

7. The Middle Screen (Diagram 13-13)

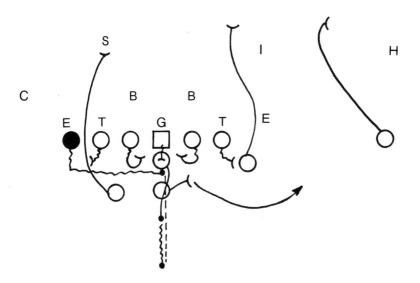

Diagram 13-13

The tight end is designated the screen receiver. The split end, slot back and left halfback release upfield and block. The two tackles block their assignments as if it is a pass. However, the center and both guards block and allow their defenders to rush the passer. The tight end blocks for two counts and quickly slides toward the middle for the screen pass. The quarterback drops for depth, scrambles, and lofts the ball over the head of the rushers to the tight end.

Sprint (Roll)-Out Screens

1. Ball Carrier to Sprint Side (Diagram 13-14)

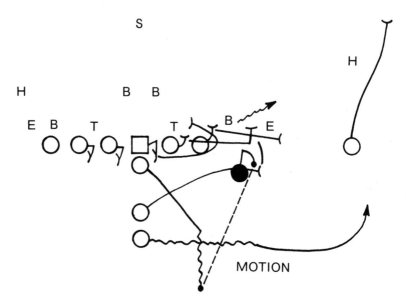

Diagram 13-14

Sprint action is shown with the fullback blocking the defensive end. The slot back starts forward, hesitates, and waits for the screen blockers. Motion is used to draw the defense toward the two receivers outside.

2. Ball Carrier Away from Sprint Side (Diagram 13-15)

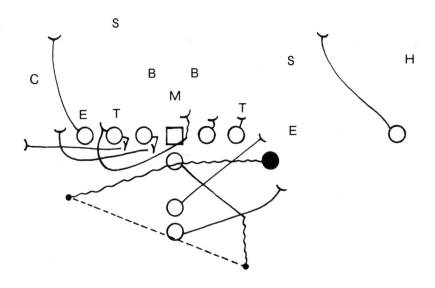

Diagram 13-15

The tight and split ends release to draw the secondary deep. The slot back holds for a count and slides across the formation in front of the screen blockers. The quarterback sprints out, pulls up, and throws back to the slot back.

3. Sprint Flood Screen (Diagram 13-16)

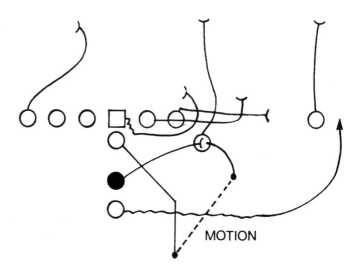

Diagram 13-16

The tailback starts in motion, setting up a three man release to the formation's strength. The quarterback sprints out, pulls up, and flips the ball to the fullback, who slips into the screen after blocking the defensive end.

Play Action Screens

   1. An Isolation Play Action Screen (Diagram 13-17)

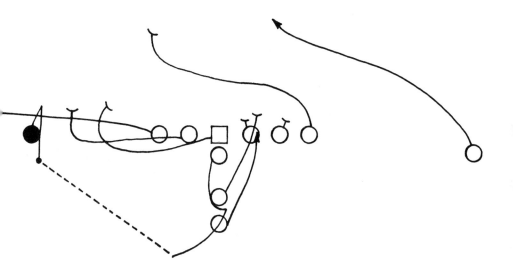

Diagram 13-17

The isolation play serves as an example of a quick screen from a play action look. The tailback and fullback fake the isolation play. The quarterback reverse pivots, delivers a good, but quick fake to the tailback, and immediately throws to the split end. The split end starts upfield, retraces his path, and waits for the football. The onside tackle, guard, and center automatically sprint as fast as possible at the snap of the football to protect the end. The tackle's role is important. As he is sprinting, he looks to either the defensive halfback responsible for the split end, or to any other defender located in the area that could stop the play.

2. Delayed Play Action (Diagram 13-18)

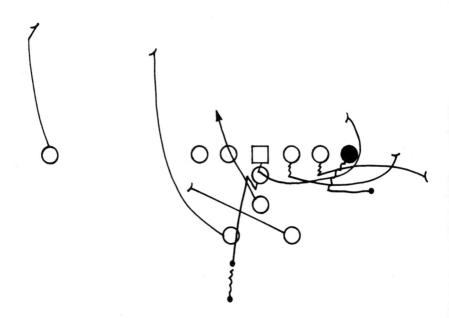

Diagram 13-18

The wishbone option attack illustrates an example of a delayed type screen. The quarterback first fakes the fullback veer. The play action pass is then faked to the split end side. As the rush develops toward the quarterback, he begins to retreat and quickly passes the ball to the screening tight end.

Index